The Best
Men's Stage Monologues
of 2002

Smith and Kraus *Books for Actors*

MONOLOGUE AUDITION SERIES

The Best Men's / Women's Stage Monologues of 2001
The Best Men's / Women's Stage Monologues of 2000
The Best Men's / Women's Stage Monologues of 1999
The Best Men's / Women's Stage Monologues of 1998
The Best Men's / Women's Stage Monologues of 1997
The Best Men's / Women's Stage Monologues of 1996
The Best Men's / Women's Stage Monologues of 1995
The Best Men's / Women's Stage Monologues of 1994
The Best Men's / Women's Stage Monologues of 1993
The Best Men's / Women's Stage Monologues of 1992
The Best Men's / Women's Stage Monologues of 1991
The Best Men's / Women's Stage Monologues of 1990
One Hundred Men's / Women's Stage Monologues from the 1980s
2 Minutes and Under: Character Monologues for Actors Volumes I and II
Monologues from Contemporary Literature: Volume I
Monologues from Classic Plays 468 BC to 1960 AD
100 Great Monologues from the Renaissance Theatre
100 Great Monologues from the Neo-Classical Theatre
100 Great Monologues from the 19th Century Romantic and Realistic Theatres
The Ultimate Audition Series Volume I: 222 Monologues, 2 Minutes & Under
The Ultimate Audition Series Volume II: 222 Monologues, 2 Minutes & Under
    from Literature

YOUNG ACTOR MONOLOGUE SERIES

Cool Characters for Kids: 71 One-Minute Monologues
Great Scenes and Monologues for Children, Volumes I and II
Great Monologues for Young Actors, Volumes I and II
Short Scenes and Monologues for Middle School Actors
Multicultural Monologues for Young Actors
The Ultimate Audition Series for Middle School Actors Vol.I: 111 One-Minute
    Monologues
The Ultimate Audition Series for Teens Vol. I: 111 One-Minute Monologues
The Ultimate Audition Series for Teens Vol.II: 111 One-Minute Monologues
The Ultimate Audition Series for Teens Vol.III: 111 One-Minute Monologues
The Ultimate Audition Series for Teens Vol.IV: 111 One-Minute Monologues
The Ultimate Audition Series for Teens Vol.V: 111 One-Minute Monologues
    from Shakespeare
Wild and Wacky Characters for Kids: 60 One-Minute Monologues

If you require prepublication information about upcoming Smith and Kraus books, you may receive our semiannual catalogue, free of charge, by sending your name and address to *Smith and Kraus Catalogue, PO Box 127, Lyme, NH 03768.* Or call us at (800) 895-4331; fax (603) 643-6431.

The Best
Men's Stage Monologues
of 2002

edited by D. L. Lepidus

MONOLOGUE AUDITION SERIES

A SMITH AND KRAUS BOOK

Published by Smith and Kraus, Inc.
177 Lyme Road, Hanover, NH 03755
www.SmithKraus.com

© 2003 by Smith and Kraus, Inc.
All rights reserved
Manufactured in the United States of America

First Edition: November 2003
10 9 8 7 6 5 4 3 2 1

Cover illustration by Lisa Goldfinger
Cover design by Julia Hill Gignoux

The Monologue Audition Series
ISSN 1067-134X
ISBN 1-57525-326-7

Contents

Foreword

If you have bought this book, or are thinking of buying this book, most likely you are a student or aspiring professional actor always in search of monologues to work on in class or to use for auditions. Or, maybe you're a teacher, looking for exciting new material for your students. It is my firm belief that the monologues in this book will suit your needs perfectly.

For one thing, they are almost all from published, readily available plays. (See Permission Acknowledgments section in the back of this book for publisher information. If the play has not been published, though, I have included information as to how to get the complete script from the author. After all, you have to read the entire play to better understand the piece you are working on.

And here's another thing, although I have included monologues for a wide range of actors, from teens to octogenarians, the lion's share are for younger actors — teens to thirties — because that's who, by and large, needs these books the most. Which is not to say that some of the pieces for older actors aren't fabulous. They are. The two monologues from Don Nigro's *November* come to mind, or one from Bill C. Davis' *Avow*. And there are some fine pieces for those of you "of a certain age" — something for everyone from Smith and Kraus!

I have tried to give a sense of each monologue's context with my brief introductions to each piece; but, inevitably, you'll have questions. Hooray! Now you can read the whole play!

Well, kids, I'm off to being work on the 2003 monologue books. Oh boy, I can't wait — hundreds of more plays to read!

— D. L. Lepidus

ALTER EGOS
Jon McGovern

Comic

This is a one-man play in which the actor plays several different roles. The other "voices" mentioned are some of the other characters we have heard. Here, the actor is something of a contemporary Romeo.

I CAN MAKE IT ON MY OWN

ACTOR: Whenever I think about you I feel halfway between Romeo and a big dork. I feel good or like Romeo when I think about how much I was in love with you. I mean, we would be talking on the phone and we'd say good-bye and I'd go to do something else and then I'd get this overwhelming feeling and I'd have to call you up again and tell you how much I was in love with you. But then I think about what you said and what you did and I feel like a big dork — because I imagine you hanging up with me and calling up some twisted two-faced girlfriend hotline . . . "Press 1 if your man loves you and you don't him. Press 2 if he just made a fool of himself over you. Press 3 if you'd like to chat with other two-faced girlfriends." "Hey, girl! Listen to wha' my man jus' did!" I know you say it's different but that's hard to believe. Yes. Yes. You say it wasn't that you didn't love me but that you realized you loved me like a friend rather than a lover . . . Now that first of all makes me feel great after all the sex we had. What? Did you roll over one night and think, I love him like a friend! Well, that certainly boosts my ego! It just makes me feel even dumber because I did love you like that . . . I . . . do. Oh I hate this! I start to get all mushy and sound like some Boyz II Men song and you know it just bounces off you! I just want to love you and you don't love me. You're beautiful, sensitive and talented and sweet and I'm just . . . well . . . wait a minute . . . What am I saying? And I'm just . . . what? Romeo the Dork? NO! You know

1

what? I'm not gonna do this anymore. Romeo certainly wouldn't have killed himself if Juliet was "just a pal." And I'm certainly not gonna be a dork the rest of my life — loving you from afar . . . I'm good-looking and sensitive and

(In the voice of Velvet.) smooth and

(Lerlene's voice.) ambitious and

(Lear's voice.) strong and

(Make-over Guerrilla's voice.) stylish and

(Zarzuffa's voice.) fabulous and . . .

and I'm funnier than you . . . OK, I use more Nutrasweet than you, but regardless . . . I deserve to have somebody who really loves me. Forget being the slacker Romeo wannabe in some sad indie film. I'm gonna be King Lear in some big, glamorous, action-packed, four and a half hour uncut Hollywood extravaganza! I know what I'm worth and like my Aunt Bertha says . . . "shit, baby! It's a lot!" So you can just find someone new to string along and torment . . . And ya know I'm not bitter . . . I know you can't say I'm not bitter without really sounding bitter . . . But it's the truth! Something clicked, maybe self-loathing overload or something . . . But I don't need you anymore. See ya, Juliet . . . this time parting is just plain sweet. I can make it my own.

(Blackout.)

A.M. SUNDAY
Jerome Hairston

Dramatic

Jay, a black teenager, is talking to his father, R.P. Jay knows about the "other woman" his father has been seeing, and he reveals this knowledge to his father.

JAY: It's not always silence. When the phone rings, and there's no one there. There was once, this one time when I heard something. This breathing. So I waited. To see if anything would be said. Was about to give up, but then I heard it. A voice. This uneven voice. One I never heard before, but still, somehow I knew she had the right number. And she asked me. She asked me this one thing. *(Pause.)* "Is your father happy?" *(Pause.)* I ain't say nothin'. I stayed quiet. I stayed. So, she asks again, "Is your father happy?" And the way she said it. So desperate. Soft. Like she. Like she was in love with you. Or needed to be in love with you. Sounded in need of something. She asks again. And this time, I was about to answer, but once I got strength up to . . . she hung up. She hung up. I've tried making sense of it. But it's a mystery. A total mystery. But those sort of things happen, I guess. Mysteries go unexplained. Phones get broken. I don't know what else to say. I don't know.

A.M. SUNDAY

Jerome Hairston

Dramatic

Jay, a black teenager, is talking to his girlfriend, Lorie (white). He has heard some other kids talking about her.

JAY: Lorie sucks nigger dick. *(Pause.)* That's what I heard. Lorie sucks nigger dick. Is it true? . . . *(Pause.)* I'm standing outside school yesterday. The sun shining. Shining like always. On everything, everywhere. I'm thinking about summer. Your green swoop and ribboned hair. Thinking so deep, I almost don't hear it. But I do. I most definitely hear. . . .

I got jealous. Angry jealous. On the hunt, wanting to know. Who this guy was, his name. And if he knew, knew about me and you. I mean, really, who the hell this nigger think he is? *(Pause.)* You know, it only took half a second. For the answer to sink in. I've had this name my whole life. But it's like I never even heard it. Till then. Suddenly the sun grows brighter. Hotter, harsher. A half-second later the world's different. That's what happens when a question and an answer come together, I guess. The world changes. It's amazing thing the first time you realize that. You start listenin' for it to change all the time. *(Pause.)* You do understand my question, right? . . .

So is it? Is it true? . . .

If you don't answer. That means you don't see me. That you never saw me. Then I'll have no choice. I'll have no choice but to hate you. To hate you deep. And that's not what I want to do. Out here. In the woods. The rain. . . .

So much gets left unsaid in this world. So much. I need it to change. No matter what it looks like after. So, just tell me. Tell me the truth. Lorie sucks nigger dick. Is it true?

AVOW

Bill C. Davis

Dramatic

Fr. Raymond, forty-two, answers Irene, a woman with whom he is sharing a burgeoning attraction, after she asks if there is any romantic relationship he trusts.

FR. RAYMOND: Actually — my mother and father. They're very romantic — still. My parents still hold hands when they're shopping, or waiting on line for a movie. My father brings my mother her morning coffee — on a tray. Always did. And I remember that they looked at each other when they talked. Even when they'd have one of their rare arguments, they'd look at each other. It mattered so much to each of them what the other one was saying. I felt left out — little brat that I was. But I don't want to give you the wrong impression. They were very good parents. They were. And to be fair, I didn't always feel left out. I remember one time — it was summer — we were working in the yard, and by accident, my mother sprayed my father with the hose. He got the hose and sprayed her back — and then they sort of tumbled to the ground laughing and then I picked up the hose and . . . I don't know — I guess I was eleven or twelve — and I sprayed the two of them. And they laughed out loud and held each other. They were completely, soaking wet — their clothes were wet and grass-stained — their hair was dripping — the sun was bright and I'm spraying them like they were on fire — and they kissed — on the mouth — right in front of me. I thought it was great. I still think that was the most romantic kiss I ever saw.

BIRTH
Bless ji Jaja

Comic

Fred is a black man in his sixties. Here he is talking to his friend and neighbor about the differences between men and women.

FRED: . . . We have one natural factor working against us. And that one factor is woman, herself. . . .

Women. Let's start with the primary years. Let's say from age eighteen and for the next twenty or so years all they do is just basically lie there. Lie there while we do all the hard work. So, that means for twenty years, they're preserving strength. Occasionally faking it, preserving more strength. And then when they don't fake it, but instead do that multi-orgasmic thing they can do, well that only all the more saps our energy. So while they're preserving, conserving, and gathering steam, what does that do for us? . . .

Yeah, wait, it gets better. They also go through their "tear it up" phase. That "hurt me, work it out, give it to me stage." And you know we can't tear nothing up. Eight-pound babies come out of there, so what damage are we really doing? And they encourage this. I tell you it's a conspiracy. That's why the Black man has high blood pressure. "Tear it up, tear it up." But do our egos say, "Hey, look here bro. Let's reconsider this." No, the ego says, let's tear, rip, and pulverize it! Yeah, right. So, now there's age forty. We're starting to go down hill, *(He waves his hand, fingers spread.)* okay, and woman are now at their sexual peak. How? Why: all that preserving of strength. Now they want it more than ever. Now that we're drained and depleted, here they are complete with elaborate shows and fantasy. I tell you, I'm on to something. Why else do women have longer life expectancies? It ain't all pork and beef. I tell you they can add choochie to that list too. Yeah, so, hey, now I ration it out.

BIRTH
Bless ji Jaja

Comic

Fred is a black man in his sixties, talking to his wife, who wishes he wouldn't watch so much TV.

FRED: No, no hold on cause you think I'm blowing hot air. Allow me to make you gain more respect so you can stop disrespecting this vital piece of furniture here. Now, let me take you back to early 19 and 63. Birmingham, Alabama, and the local police commissioner, Bull Connor. Now picture attack dogs, fire hoses, mace, and swinging batons. Scenes of brutality and racial intolerance. Now when those scenes were finally shown on what, the television? The tel-e-vis-ion did things start to change? Yes, they did. Decent Americans saw it and folks worldwide were outraged. The Kennedys saw it. They all saw it via television and what came with it but all the sympathy, support, and moral outrage. By spring those televised demonstrations led to national legislation which led to what? The de-seg-re-gation of restrooms, water fountains, lunch counters, theaters, and more importantly for you, what? I know I don't have to remind you, what? What were you celebrating? The desegregation of what? . . .

Fitting rooms! So you wouldn't have to buy a dress, come home, try it on, have it not look like it does on those anorexic window mannequins, and then you not be able to take it back. No wonder you're such a good seamstress. And so, to what do we owe the end of that indignity? Tel-e-vision. So what do I have in my living room? What do I sit in front of to pay tribute and commemorate those hard-fought achievements? Not a fire hydrant. Not a dog leash. But what? A big screen, remote control, picture-in-picture, Technicolor, tel-e-vision. . . . My television. It keeps me informed. It let's me know what struggles are still to be fought.

BLIND HARASSMENT
Gordon Sumlak-Langlois

Dramatic

> *This is a play that examines "harassment" in many forms. Here, a man (called simply "Husband") is discussing with a lawyer filing a same-sex harassment suit.*

HUSBAND: Imagine it from my perspective. My wife and I go on a cruise to Alaska . . . a second honeymoon. She's never been up there but she really enjoyed the time she spent in the Canadian Rockies. You know . . . she started talking about Banff, Lake Louise, glaciers, that kind of stuff. And I thought it would be great to go back up there . . . 'cause I hadn't been there since I left Alaskis, so what the hell, right? So we're there in Anchorage, eating in such and such restaurant. The nicest place in town. Nothing compared to what we have here, but nice. Well anyways, there is this bar that's up a couple of feet from the sunken floor of the restaurant. Well, we're having a wonderful first night when an argument breaks out at the bar. My back was to the commotion, but I could hear what was going on. There are these two guys picking on this man sitting alone at the other side of the bar. They're yelling insults at him, calling him dick sucker, queer, makin' comments about what he would sound like while being done up the butt . . . stuff like that. They sounded pretty drunk. I was trying to ignore them and focus on my wife and my glass of red wine. But by the end of it, these two assholes had the attention of everyone there . . . the management, all the customers and waiters . . . even some of the kitchen staff came out. So I turn as these two guys are bein' escorted outside and . . . and we lock eyes — for a second. Then he smirks at me . . . just enough so I can see his gold tooth. . . . That night, I woke up screaming . . . Sweating. It woke Sarah up. I couldn't sleep. At first, the nightmares were just flashbacks. But then . . . then . . . it was like I was still working there. Like it was continuing. I saw myself eating lunch and they would rip my pants off or chase me down the corridors. I was constantly scared. Looking behind me, hiding around corners, afraid to turn down empty hallways. Each time, it got worse. They were everywhere and I couldn't escape them.

BOYS AND GIRLS
Tom Donaghy

Seriocomic

Jason, a gay man in his twenties to thirties, is confronting his ex-boyfriend Reed, who left him a while ago but then has wanted to get together again (as "friends"??).

JASON: You can't do that. You can't anymore. Calling me. And some set place. Some agreement we come to and showing up at a certain time only to — to — you can't. That's it. I don't want the keys anymore. *(He throws his keys on the floor.)* It's too easy. It's this thing that we should be sure we're thinking. I don't want to be in intimate situations and not have thought behind them. Not be conscious, not consciously know what we're doing. And fuck you! Fuck me? Fuck you! I am fine. I'm fine. I'm sitting there fine at my desk and you call and make plans?! Fuck you. Like nothing's happened. Six months now! Something's happened and fuck you. Everyone knows. My friends say this is *nothing*. No reason at all. You overreacted and then, what, I have to come meet you in some place you've found in what, Zagats? And sit there and eat hummus? I don't like hummus, it dries me out! And I'm meeting you places like we're still together when we are not. And getting into this whole thing that you start — and I'm just getting clear in my head — you know — and every time I start to get clear you call me up. And I don't call you — you call me. I'm sitting there fine, at my desk doing well. Everyone there says my work is excellent. That's what they say and you call me. You call me . . . You shit. What about me? Those shirts, that closet full of shirts for who? No one else likes them. You're the only one who likes me in blues and purples!

BOYS AND GIRLS
Tom Donaghy

Seriocomic

Jason, a gay man in his twenties to thirties, is confronting his ex-boyfriend Reed, who left him a while ago but then has wanted to get together again (as "friends"??).

JASON: He's — he's — he likes his work. He's a consultant on parks. How they should be arranged. Where the fountains go. . . .

How they look at night with the lights, the shrubs, are there're enough benches. Or too many. What style. We have all these models at home, little benches like in a dollhouse. He carves them. I move them around when he's late and I'm mad. And, you know, I didn't know people like him existed — I guess I thought there were just parks! But there are consultants on them and it's very precise and everybody comes in and dickers over everything for months and months, sometimes years. A lot of times years. There's one just got finished he took me to the week we met. And we had a picnic. *(Beat.)* I shouldn't — . . . *(Beat.)* He's um — he's um — . I need water. *(He goes into the bathroom and continues from there.)* He's close to his family. And they're okay, they're Southerners. So they eat and say "y'all." I mean they're not hicks. They're not with pickup trucks on cement blocks in the yard or anything. They're respectful and treat me like, um, when we've gone down, like some kind of dignitary. *(He returns with a glass of water.)* Some exotic person from a faraway place, you know, that they've been told they should treat well. And they do. And they do. . . .

Which is where he gets it. I don't want to do this if you're going to be sad. . . .

I don't want to make you sad.

CARL THE SECOND
Marc Palmieri

Comic

> *Carl, a man in his thirties who works in a used bookstore, is telling us*
> *about a dream he recently had. He was the hero of his dream.*

CARL: *(To audience.)* It was getting exciting. We practiced every couple of
days. We lost our shortstop to the touring company of *Annie Get Your
Gun*, but replaced him with a guy who had been in *Cats*. We weren't
a great team man for man, but something scrappy and hearty was
developing. It was all I could think about. *The Vindicators*. How perfect a name. I thought of nothing else. The game. Day and night.
The game. I would stay late in the store reading baseball books about
great games in history, famous underdogs, the wisdom of Yogi Berra,
the shot heard round the world, the curse of the Bambino. One night
I fell asleep and dreamt I was in the late innings of our game. We
were losing one nothing. All of us were dressed in sharp, bright pin-
striped uniforms and there must have been ten thousand people
watching from the bleachers. In the dream. Al had a two-hitter going,
and when Lance got up a deafening boo came from the rowdy home
crowd. Christine was in the stands. So were my parents. They held
up a sign that read CARL IS NUMBER ONE. Al blew two under-
handed heaters right by Lance, but on the third, he swung and sent
a blazing line drive deep into the right center gap. I gave chase.
Sprinted for it, glove open, arms outstretched, dove, but missed it
by an inch. Lance rounded the bases and stepped triumphantly on
home plate. I laid out in the grass, spent, exhausted, slain. My friends
ran to my aid as the weeping crowd began chanting my name in sympathy. Carl! Carl! Carl! It was ecstasy. I struggled to regain my stance,
when something changed in the dream. I looked down and found
I was standing on the hard wooden deck of a boat, rocking gently
in a dark, vast ocean. It was cold and foggy and gloomy. I looked
around and saw that instead of my teammates, I was surrounded by
the most interesting collection of literary characters ever assembled.

CRUISING CLOSE TO CRAZY
Laura Shaine Cunningham

Dramatic

Chase (thirties to fifties) is a very suave, very macho country western musician. Here he is talking to Carolee, whom he would consider to be a "girl singer."

CHASE: Don't argue with me, Carolee. I didn't come to continue the fight. I just come to set the record straight . . . *(He shuts his eyes, rocks, as if in contained pain.)* I didn't think you would do me the way you done. . . .

One, I didn't think you'd take off with my drummer. Two, I didn't think you'd bad-mouth me in a song. Three, I didn't think you'd run out on me when I needed you. And four, I didn't expect you'd sue me! . . .

And I made up my mind, after that last tour, that there's two things I will never do again, and that's drink while I'm on tour, and sleep with a girl singer. That would never happen to me now . . . be fooled the way I was . . . And it wouldn't have happened to me then, if I hadn't been drinking. But I haven't had a drink in *(He pauses for emphasis.)* forty-four days, in order to be ready for tonight and my head is real clear now and I see everything, the way it was . . . and is. *(He takes a toke from the joint.)* I don't know why I had to go around anesthetized the way I did. I must have been in even more pain than I knew . . . *(Eyeing Carolee in utter hurt.)* But you. I didn't think you would do me like you done. I had to cut a single to get rid of the bad feelings . . . I was going to sing it tonight. . . .

I almost died. . . .

You can kick a man only so hard, when he's down. If you ask me to forgive you, I know, Lord that I should. I should turn the other cheek but I don't know if I have that kind of strength. I only know . . . *(Sweet, meek look.)* I'm trying.

THE DEAD EYE BOY
Angus MacLachlan

Dramatic

Billy (twenties to thirties) is a recovering drug addict. This monologue is a direct address to the audience. This is the first part of a much longer monologue — in case you need something longer . . .

BILLY: I got to say. Today I'm grateful. 'Cause. Um . . . Well, I'll go ahead now. *(He sighs, and laughs a little, nervously.)* This morning at work. I got this boss, says we can't get off our machines till someone relieves us. But I — I says, enough of that, and went out back behind the building — just to have a smoke. . . . So — I got this whole macho thing going on in my head — you know, I'm conducting this dialogue with myself: "You . . . so-and-so," I say, "You're not a man letting him eat your . . . " you know. I'm confused and don't know what. And all of a sudden I look down, and right there at my feet was some pharmaceuticals, and works. In the dumpster. Right there at my feet. All wrapped up, pretty. . . . Unbelievable. And — man — I mean to tell you. It was like Christmas. . . . Or Easter. . . . My heart racing, I picked 'em up. I did. And I held 'em. A year ago? Six months ago? Olden times, I'd a'picked up a syringe on the road, rubbed it on a matchbook and used it no matter how dirty it was. And these were — . . . Like an answered prayer. At that moment. *(He pauses.)* It rocked me. What was it doing here? Why did I find it, at that minute when I was all — mixed up? But. Now. Here's the thing. Wait — I made a choice. By the grace of God I put 'em back. I put 'em down, y'all. I left 'em. *(He takes a deep breath.)* I hightailed it back inside, and I saw my boss and I gave him a big "Hello sir!" — big "blank"-eating grin on my face. And I went to my station and worked my behind off. All day. Like a real person. 'Cause, that's what I am now. A real person. And I'm here to tell you, I never thought I would be. Listen — I got normal problems. You know? . . . I got a new wife — not that that's a problem. Honey. But I got a truck payment, and a teenager, and a boss that makes my butt walk barbed wire. I can't hardly believe it. I got a home. Y'all. A home. Now if that's not proof there is a God, I don't know what it. *(He stops a second.)* But I thought about that package in the dumpster all day. Don't think I didn't. Man . . . Here I am. And, when I think about where I come from.

THE DEAD EYE BOY
Angus MacLachlan

Dramatic

> *Billy (twenties to thirties) is a recovering drug addict, speaking in an addicts' support group meeting.*

BILLY: My name is Billy, I'm an addict . . .I don't know if this is exactly related to drugs, but. Well I . . . I'm losing my. A part of me is. I'm out of a job. Last day at the factory was Friday. But — things are going alright . . . *(He stops himself from cowering.)* Well . . . It's a little rough. *(He pauses, then speaks slowly.)* Hell . . . the dream came back. Some of y'all may have heard it before. But . . . in it I'm young. Just driving, just started. And I'm high. I feel great. It's a great high. Warm. The "bubble." But. I'm driving down the highway and I lose control and I hit another car — and it bursts into flame. Then I see this man rush out of the other car, screaming. And he — he runs around trying to open the other door 'cause. 'Cause his baby's in the back seat. And the car's burning . . . I get really scared, then. Really rocked. I'm just a kid, and I've messed up, you know. Bad. I panic. And I leave. So they don't know who hit 'em . . . But as I'm flying away I see in the rearview the man pulling a black thing from the car. And I see it move. It's his baby. Burnt. Black. Like coal. But still alive . . . Then it's later. The baby lived. I see it. But it doesn't have no face, or hands. Just — its face is a mask. Like, scar tissue and eyes. Screaming from the pain, and growing up . . . And the only form of power the — the boy — has as he's going through all the pain — is his voice — the only thing that gets through — is when he's screaming — to his father, or crying. Pleading, "Please be gentle. Please be gentle." . . . And I know this. I did this . . . *(He pauses again.)* He's pushing me for something he wants. They threw him out of school, he's testing everybody. He's acting out. Drugs . . . I know it — exactly. *(He pauses.)* I want to hit him. I see him, I think about the anger I felt at his age. It's like looking at myself and I'm so angry with him. He makes me feel like I'm . . . I'm my dad. I want to beat the hell out of him. He's driving his mother — Oh, she's got a little cold. She didn't feel up to coming tonight. *(He stops himself again.)* . . . Well, she's at loose ends . . . We're scrambling, y'all. I'm out of one job. And not bringing anything in. We got rent, and insurance, you know. It's a tough time. *(He stops.)* Tough time. Temptations. *(He can't go on, and consciously "covers" with some optimism.)* . . . We'll be OK, though. Thanks for letting me share. *(He finishes and leans forward, ready to listen to someone else. One knee bounces, though, and he's still preoccupied.)*

DEFILED
Lee Kalcheim

Comic

> *Harry is a librarian who's gone over the edge. In the original produc-*
> *tion he was played by Jason Alexander. Probably, he's about forty. Here,*
> *he is talking to a detective named Brian Dickey, who's hoping to stop*
> *Harry from blowing up the library.*

HARRY: . . . Let's try looking under . . . "Famine." Maybe I'm doing a paper
about "The Politics of Hunger." So I type in "Famine" . . . No I'll
even be more specific . . . I'll type "Famine, Ireland." *(Types.)* And I
get . . . *(Reads:)* "1. Famine in Ulster, The Regional Impact, 2. Famine
in Waterford 1845–1850, 3. Famine in Zimbabwe, 4. Famine in Ben-
gal." Then a space and "Your entry Famine in Ireland would be here."
Ah! So there's no such listing. I got close . . . Famine in Ulster. But
I'm not going to find "A Modest Proposal" here. . . .

   I'm an undereducated student who has never heard of "A Modest Proposal." I don't know the title. I don't know it exists. I want
the damn library to lead me to it so I can discover it! What the hell
good is this machine if it can't help me? *(He gives it a swat and walks
away, turns.)* When you walked into my father's store and said to him,
"I need a tool to fix my thing-a-ma-jig," he'd say . . . "Ah . . . well .
. . try this . . . and if this doesn't work try this in combination with
this!" You are lost in repair-your-house hell and my dad rescues you.
Today you go into a Home Depot, the store the size of a football
field. First you search for a salesman in this abyss. Then ask him if
he knows anything about "thing-a-ma-jigs." He says . . . "No . . . I
sell telephones." So, you wander around in this discount jungle trying to find a man who hopefully can help you . . . to find the tool
to fix your house. If you do find another salesman, unlike my father
in his over-stuffed old store, he doesn't know who you are. Doesn't
particularly care and doesn't know how to get what you need. It has

never occurred to some dolt sitting in a windowless room somewhere in East Japip, copying cards into the database that we need help! They leave it to US to do the work. They leave it to us to spend hours searching the database for the books we need. Plodding through the jungle, hoping to come to the clearing. These old, clunky card catalogues do it for us! Zap! They are our Map! These computers are sending students out into the jungle without a map. This is the age of information age and we are less informed than a novice in a medieval monastery. We are undereducated and over entertained. This is progress? This is insanity!

DEFILED
Lee Kalcheim

Comic

Harry is a librarian who's gone over the edge. In the original production he was played by Jason Alexander. Probably, he's about forty. Here, he is talking to a detective named Brian Dickey, who's hoping to stop Harry from blowing up the library.

HARRY: You should go. Before it looks like America. Before they clean up all the sweet little villages and build malls. . . .

Go now! Before it disappears. Just like this . . . this library will disappear. . . .

It won't disappear like that. *(Snaps fingers.)* The slow death started with the administrators, like Stockerfield wanting to get rid of the files to "clean up the place." The files go eventually . . . there'll be no library. Just a little store that's like a take-out restaurant. There'll be stores on the street where you go and order a book. Like Chinese food. Like a burger. You wait, they give it to you. You go home. No grand vaulted ceilinged room to sit in. No long shiny tables to sit at. No echoing footsteps. No essence of place that gives books the holiness they should rightly have. It's just a Burger. You want it. You got it. Well . . . that's if we're lucky enough to have even that. With the Internet we won't have books at all. You'll just order a book up on your screen. Print it out or read it right there in the dark in the privacy of your smelly little office. After several generations we'll forget what it feels like to turn a page. To fall asleep with a book on our chest, to carry a book with you that you're hooked on wherever you go so you can read it between stops on the subway. The whole thrilling tactile experience of reading a book, pages designed by typesetting artists. Print picked by editors and authors. Dedications, prefaces and notes and even the color of the paper. Each decision making each book a mini work of art. This cannot be found on a screen. A screen is dead. A book is alive. In eighty years, four generations, no one will know the difference. *(He sits, remembering.)* I . . . I once saw the original manuscript of Henry James' *Washington Square* in the rare book room at New York Public Library. I trembled when I held it. I touched pages he had touched and felt his energy. I saw his notes in the margins. I understand how he wrote it because of how he rewrote it. When I held that manuscript, I learned something about the man and the time and the art of writing and my own vulnerability to heroes. That will be gone. It will all be gone. These, them, those *(He indicates the books, the table, the library.)* will all be gone. *(He takes a deep breath to hold back his emotions.)* You want to live in that world?

THE DYING GAUL
Craig Lucas

Dramatic

Robert, a gay man in his thirties, has recently helped his terminally ill lover to die, and he has serious guilt issues with that, which he is sharing with a doctor named Foss.

ROBERT: . . . When the morphine didn't work, and I realized how long it was going to take, even if I could convince those bozos to withhold fluids, obviously his brain was destroyed, the drains weren't working, filling his skull with antibiotics which were doing nothing at all, he was literally producing that goop from his brain . . . and it was at least another week before you were going to get back from Fiji, I'm not blaming you . . . I called around, and someone, a nurse's aide, told me that there was something kept on nurses' carts — potassium chloride, which if I injected it directly into the IV would stop his heart: instantly. The aide warned me that he could wake up from the coma . . . which he did. His eyes flying open . . . after a week, brain-dead . . . And he shouted . . . a sound more than a word . . . just like that pig . . . And I have been thinking. See?, I'm bad, I did the wrong thing . . . that it was for me, because I couldn't stand watching it. So, and you gave me permission. What kind of Buddhist gives somebody morphine, why didn't you just give me a gun? . . . *(Pause.)* There. *(Pause.)* I should have told you . . . *(Pause.)* That's . . . You ask how big my rage is. That's . . . Everyone should — World War Three, that's what I want. Not just Auschwitz . . . not . . . The whole planet. All of us . . . I want the world, all mankind. We should all . . . hear that. We should all know what that's like. *(Pause.)* Yes. You were useless to me. You were useless to Malcolm. At the end. Thank you for trying, but . . . *(Pause.)* You were really worth nothing. Nothing.

THE FATHER CLOCK
Walter Wykes

Comic

> The Father Clock *is a rather "absurdist" comedy about two actors and a stage manager who have been abandoned by their director. Now, they have to pull the show together themselves. Here Snub, the younger of the two actors, is talking to the older actor and the stage manager.*

SNUB: Listen to me! Listen! Your . . . your mind is clouded right now. OK? You're not thinking clearly. We have to get away from here. That's all. Away from *him!* And then everything will fall back into place! Like a dream! Like . . . like waking up and finding what's real! *(Pause.)* I found an old play. *(He pulls a very old, cloth-covered book from his shirt.)* It's one you've never read. It was supposed to have been burned years ago — along with all of its kind — it didn't fit the director's vision. But somehow . . . it survived! An original copy! I found it in an old bookstore! They didn't know what they had! I . . . I was waiting to give it to you . . . waiting for just the right moment . . . but now . . . now I . . . here. *(He offers her the book.)* Please . . . please take it. *(Pause.)* Please? *(Pause.)* We'll . . . we'll read it together. OK? It will open your eyes to a . . . a whole new world! A whole new language of the stage! A forgotten language! We'll . . . we'll talk about what it means . . . about . . . about our real feelings. We'll have meaningful discussions. And . . . and one day . . . we'll wake up . . . and everything will be just . . . just like it used to be.

THE FATHER CLOCK
Walter Wykes

Comic

> The Father Clock *is a rather "absurdist" comedy about two actors and a stage manager who have been abandoned by their director. Now, they have to pull the show together themselves. Here Flub, an older actor, expresses his dismay at being abandoned by the director.*

FLUB: No! How . . . how could he leave us? Now! When we need him most! He . . . he said he'd always be here! Until the end of time! He . . . he promised. *(Pause.)* And now . . . he's . . . it's all . . . it's all falling apart . . . and he's not . . . he's not here to . . . to put it all . . . *(Pause.)* WHERE IS HE? *(Pause.)* He must . . . he must be on his way! He's been held up! That's all! Caught in traffic! The streets are empty, I admit, but . . . all of those lights . . . some of them still work, and he's . . . he's probably . . . oh wait . . . I've got it! He's found another theater! That's it! A new space! And he wanted to surprise us! Oh, how exciting! We've been acting like such babies! He'll have a good laugh at our expense, won't he? I can't wait to see! A new stage! It must be something wonderful! Not like this one! This husk! No! This is only a shadow! A mustard seed! Why it's . . . it's probably beyond our ability to grasp! Something magnificent for once! A . . . a single site! With no partition! No barrier! No auditorium! . . . One space! All of us together! A hundred thousand swiveling seats! Always a full house! And lots of clapping! Clapping and laughter! And . . . and lights! Oh! Lights! All kinds of luminous vibrations! Fresnels of gold shooting light in waves, in sheets, in fusillades of fiery arrows! A living theater! It's going to be something! He must be on his way! Right now! To tell us! To let us know! I'm going to tell him all of the silly ideas we've passed around! We'll all have a good laugh! All of us! A nice little chuckle! He's . . . he's probably at the door right now! There! That cough! Did you hear it? I'd know that cough anywhere! We have to give him a great welcome.

FORTUNE'S FOOL
Ivan Turgenev. Adapted/
translated by Mike Poulton

Seriocomic

> *Kuzovkin (played by Alan Bates in the Broadway production) is an im-*
> *poverished middle-aged gentleman who has been living off the charity*
> *of the owner of a country estate for years. The owner has recently died.*
> *His host's young daughter, recently married, has inherited the estate, and*
> *Kuzovkin's position there is far from secure. Here, we are at a luncheon*
> *in honor of the arrival of Olga and her new husband, and Kuzovkin,*
> *easily made to play the fool, has become more than a little tipsy.*

KUZOVKIN: Why? Why! Why do you torture me? What harm have I done
to anyone? . . .

A little thing? Is it a little thing, Pavel Nikolaitch? . . . The day
you arrive — the first day! *(His voice breaks.)* This is how you treat
a poor man you called your guest. Fortune has broken me, Pavel
Nikolaitch . . . Is it necessary that you should trample upon my head?
Shame on you, sir! If you knew how much joy I felt when I saw your
love for Olga Petrovna . . . and hers for you . . . Why have you destroyed me, sir? Was it kindly done? . . .

And you, sir — shut your mouth, sir — you infamous, fatu-
ous, fop — nobody's addressing you, so have the goodness to take
yourself off. You think you've made a fool of me, but at what cost
to your own character, sir — we all see what you are . . . It's to you
I'm speaking, Pavel Nikolaitch. I who was your father-in-law's fool.
He thought that for a place at his table and a cast-off suit or two he
had the right to treat me like an animal — it was more shame to
him than it was to me — swine that he was. And are you swine like him,
sir? Are you like that? The manners of the court — is this how men
behave in St. Petersburg? Well, shame on the lot of you! . . .

Drunk, am I? Play fair, Pavel Nikolaitch, who made me drunk? Oh, forget it, forget me . . . You've had your fun — first day you arrive and I'm back in my place — a laughingstock — face in the custard . . . But there's something I could tell you all that would wipe the smiles from your faces . . .

FORTUNE'S FOOL
Ivan Turgenev. Adapted/
translated by Mike Poulton

Seriocomic

Kuzovkin (played by Alan Bates in the Broadway production) is an impoverished middle-aged gentleman who has been living off the charity of the owner of a country estate for years. Here, he reveals to Olga, the young woman who has recently inherited the estate, the truth about who he really is.

KUZOVKIN: I think . . . How would I truly judge? I know nothing except by feeling — but I think the truth is that her sanity began to fail. She would go into the icon room and stand crossing herself before the holy images. Smiling sometimes. And all the time my heart was aching for her sorrows. She could hardly eat. Nobody spoke to her except me. The servants moved about the house like ghosts. Can you imagine that? That strange unnatural silence. In the evening she would talk to me — in here, this room — and it was all about him . . . until one night, suddenly it was as if her love for him had broken. She turned to me, and looked at me, and after a long, long silence when I could feel my heart beating as though it would explode in my breast — I loved her so hopelessly — and I knew . . . I knew . . . what she was going to say, and oh . . . quite suddenly, and calmly she said: "Vassily Semyonitch, I know how deeply and purely you love me, and I know at last that he has never loved me, and that he will never feel anything for me but contempt and loathing . . . But I feel for you . . . I need . . ." And she laid her head on my breast . . . And, oh Olya! I didn't know what to say or do. We were both lost. Forgive me, please forgive me. I can't tell you any more about it. It's not right that I should. . . .

The very next day . . . As soon as it began to grow light I went out into the fields. I remember the skylarks. I was still in a dream. Somebody brought the news — rode over from the next village. Your father had fallen from his horse. They'd carried his body into a priest's house. I watched your mother go off in the carriage. Dear Lord, we thought she would go mad. She was hardly alive herself — right up until the time you were born. And then, as you know, she never recovered — it was as if, for the rest of her life, she inhabited some other, better world. *(He sinks.)* . . .

(Shaken.) Merciful God! Proof? Olga Petrovna, I have proof of nothing — there is no proof! That I would dare! Had I not made such a fool of myself yesterday the truth would have gone with me to my grave. I'd sooner have died. Why the good Lord did not strike me down in my folly I shall never know. Until yesterday not a soul . . . I would not even whisper it to my own soul . . . Dear God!

When your father — that man died, I tried to run away, but I was such a coward. It would have been the right thing to do, but I could not leave her, I could not break from her. And then I was afraid. The world out there terrifies me. Poverty, unkindness, the insolence of life. So, God forgive me, I did nothing. Oh, do not mistake me, dear Olya. I did not continue to hope . . . In those days, months after his death I never saw your mother. She locked herself away. She locked her mind — shut out the world. Only Praskovya Ivanova, her maid . . . And later on, and I swear this before God, I was too little of a man to dare to look her in the face. There are no proofs, Olga Petrovna, of anything.

But what were you thinking? That I should dare to use . . . Olga Petrovna, whatever men may say of me, I was born a gentleman and I have tried to honor my birth. I would never, never repeat my folly. Had you not insisted — but please never imagine that you will hear of this again. Nobody will believe the words of a fool and nor should you. Tell yourself that it's all lies, the ramblings of a man losing his mind. Make that your truth.

FOUR
Christopher Shinn

Dramatic

Dexter, about twenty, is a low-level drug dealer, on a date with Abigail, sixteen.

DEXTER: . . . I love the fireworks. In the sky like that. That's unreal. That don't happen every day. Everybody standing there, all these people, under the bridge, on the water, standing there, or sitting on their blankets, looking up at the sky, everyone looking up at the sky like that, all quiet as it goes up and then cheering when it explodes and shit. Man, I love that. That don't happen every day, you get all the people into the city like that, all of us who living out of the city go back in, and you got all the people, all looking up at the sky, and I know you say that there be, like, drunk people and kids running around being assholes, and niggers with guns and Latin Kings with knives and white boys with baseball bats and shit, but once the shit starts, you know, *everybody* stops. *Everybody* look up at the sky. And is like . . . you know? Everybody's looking up there. *(Silence. He starts dribbling.)* Anyway, you don't wanna go, that's cool, maybe we can see the sky get all bright from here, like the clouds lighting up or something, that's cool too . . . you just wanna be alone all the time, I had a grandmother like that, that's cool, only she didn't get that way 'til she got old . . . I loved coming to high school here. I loved it. Everybody loved me. I walked down the hall and everybody loved me. Only thing I didn't like was confession. They made us go to confession. I had to kneel there, it was the only time I felt stupid, all the other times felt great. Everyone knew who I was, I played *basketball,* I was the leading *scorer,* they wrote about me in the *newspaper.* Confession was the only bad thing, I hated confession, I hated doing that. You believe in God? . . . I believe in God. I don't know why you wouldn't. My dad didn't believe in God. . . .

(Beat.) I don't pray or nothing. I don't kneel down at my bed and *pray,* but a lot of things have happened to me, you know, in my life, a lot of moments, you know, and I'm always thinking God, I mean I don't look up at the sky or nothing, but I'm always thinking God, God, God, man, God brother help me out, God man what you doin', God man look at me, you know, I mean, I don't go to church or nothing.

FOUR
Christopher Shinn

Dramatic

Joe, forty, is a black married man who is actually a closeted homo-sexual. Here he is talking to a sixteen-year-old boy he has met in an Internet chat room.

JOE: I do volunteer work. I see a lot of kids in trouble these days. Sad kids. We didn't seem to be that sad when I was growing up. We learned to keep a lot inside. We didn't expect too much. In some ways, I think that was a good thing, you know? Anyway, I do this volunteer work a couple days a week, it's at the university, and the other day I was with this man, he was very poor, he was on food stamps and welfare, he was white, and he just — well he'd just had it. He was a little older than me, and he'd graduated from high school but had never gone to college, and he'd had a family — can you hear me in there? . . .

He'd had a family, and he'd lost his family, he'd left them, and then he married another woman, and he left her too, and then stopped trying to be married, decided he didn't want to be married, wanted to be on his own, wanted to do what he wanted to do. The work I do — it's a counseling center — it's a health center — I see a lot of kids. It's a surprise to see an older person. Especially a man. Anyhow — and I was talking to this man. And he's there to get his blood tested, he lives on the Berlin Turnpike, I forget which motel, one of them, and we're talking and as we're talking, I'm starting to realize . . . *(Joe takes off his sweater, revealing an undershirt.)* I'm starting to remember this man. From a bar. A gay bar. I am convinced it is he, because the man I knew, this is during the early 80s, and I was going through a rough point at that time — good thing about the disease is that it's made most people start thinking about sex instead of just having it, you know what I'm saying — made people

31

think about the other *person*, what they might have *inside* them, hidden away, invisible, which can only be a good thing *I* think, *I* think in many ways this disease is the best thing that could have happened to gay men because in a certain sense it's made us *human* — but I could go on forever about that, I'm getting away from the story. Can you hear me? Are you interested? I'll stop. I'll stop talking. . . .

Well I realized that this was the first man I'd ever slept with. Because I remember he had a scar on the bottom of his left ear that looked like, well to me, then, in that dim light, looked like a snake I remember thinking — *(The shower goes off. Joe adjusts the volume of his voice. He checks to make sure the shades are closed and the door is locked during the following.)* — I didn't bring it up with him, of course, and I looked different so I was sure he wouldn't recognize me — and what I found interesting in a purely *theoretical* way was — well I started thinking about the myths of first love — first sex — how for gay boys today getting one's first AIDS test is equivalent to the straight boy losing his virginity —

GOOD BUSINESS

Tom Gannon

Comic

Set in a dingy bar in Detroit, this is a comedy about two hustlers. Here, near the start of the play, Frank, twenties, is talking to John (same age).

FRANK: OK, OK, I'll answer your questions in a minute and tell you everything about tonight. Guillermo's not with us tonight, ah, someone else is taking his place, he had other business, it's — I'll explain it all. But first, I gotta tell you this joke. . . .

This joke, this joke I heard. It's good, it's funny, and, it's also got a little lesson in it. . . .

It's funny, it's funny. You'll like it. All right? All right. OK, so there's these two guys stranded on an island after a shipwreck. One single guy and one guy with his wife. . . .

Yeah, the wife too. So they're there for a while, you know, a few months, and the single guy is getting really horny. He wants to get a piece of the other guy's wife and she's kind of flirty, she seems like she'd do it, but the husband is always breathing down her neck. So this one day the single guy is sitting in the top of a palm tree. He's up there, taking his turn looking out at the ocean, looking for passing ships to rescue them, but he's thinking about how he's gonna fuck this woman. Then he gets this idea, he looks down at the couple on the beach and yells, "Hey you two! Stop that fucking!" And the two of them just look at each other wondering what the hell he's talking about because they're sitting ten feet apart. *(Pause.)* So the husband goes up in the tree the next day to take his turn as lookout. He's looking out at the ocean, doesn't see any ships, then he looks down at the beach, at his wife and the guy who HAD been sitting apart when he climbed up, and he says, "I'll be damned. From up here it really looks like they're fucking." . . .

But I didn't tell you that to make you laugh. I was hoping you'd find it funny, but that was a side benefit. Kind of like TV. It's only a coincidence that we are entertained by television. Television exists solely for advertisements, for companies to push cute slogans and catchy jingles — ...

Oh yeah, I'm trying to show you that from far away, if you yell loud enough, you might — you can, you can convince someone that things are one way even though they're not.

GOOD BUSINESS
Tom Gannon

Seriocomic

This play is a wild comedy about crime gone wrong. This monologue is delivered by John, who is in his twenties. He is talking to another hustler in a bar.

JOHN: . . . but see, West Bloomfield, that's way the fuck out there, man. And we're robbin' a Jew? Christ. Jesus fuckin' Christ. Do you know what they'll do to us if we get caught? Huh? We're talking a huge difference between pulling a job here, where the cops got bigger fish to fry, and out there where they'd nail our asses to the wall because we crossed the Eight Mile border. Those suburb faggots take down anything from Detroit as hard as they can, black or white — and don't think we'd get off easier because we're white. Fuck no. They'd probably come down on us twice as hard. They want us to stay on our side and they'll stay on theirs and it'll all be all right, but once anyone from HERE tries to do some business out THERE it's fuckin' showtime. Fuckin' Showtime at the Apollo. They think they gotta make an example of us. No man, I don't like it. I think we should stay on this side of Eight Mile. *(Pause.)* It's just good business.

JERRY AND TOM
Rick Cleveland

Seriocomic

> *Jerry and Tom, two hit men, are watching TV with a character referred to as "Elvis Sideburns" (thirties to forties), who claims to have been on intimate terms with the actress in the movie they're watching.*

ELVIS SIDEBURNS: You see that woman — up here on the screen? . . .
The blond, Vicki Torrance. . . .
That's my Vicki. The next part — watch this . . .
See the way she took those punches. Now that's acting. Did all her own stunts, too. . . .
I loved her more than life itself, friend. She was my fiancée.
. . . I'll tell you what happened. We fell in love. We were gonna get married. But we got mixed up with some fellers. The wrong fellers. We got in over our heads with these fellers. We went to the police. But they got to her anyway. There was an "accident" on the set. *Sudden Extreme Justice 2.* They switched a dummy flame-thrower for the real thing, and Vicki had on this flammable beehive hairdo wig. You don't wanna know. So they fixed me up with a new identity, a new job — just like they did with Elvis. Yep. He went and got himself mixed up with the wrong fellers just like me and Vicki, and they moved him up to Kalamazoo. And now here we are. A whole brand-new life. A life without the King. A life without my Vicki. One of these days they'll find me. You two fellers might even be the ones. But you see, I don't really care anymore. *(Beat.)* Look at her. This was the last thing she did. Seen it thirty-seven times. Sometimes, watching her up there like this, I forget. It's almost like she's still alive. And when she does the trick with the grenade launcher — my heart rolls over sideways and just about quits. This is all I have of her. *(Beat.)* You know what really gets me though? Not the shower scene coming up — and that's no body double, let me tell you in advance.

That's her appendix scar, those are her moles. No, what gets me is the scene where she's down in the basement. She's just sitting there, cleaning her Uzi. There's this close-up, she wipes the sweat from her face and you can see the little hairs on her arm. That really gets me. Every time. She was the love of my life. I miss her. And I don't give a shit about that much of anything anymore.

JERRY AND TOM
Rick Cleveland

Dramatic

Tom, a hit man, is on the phone to his son's school. Apparently, they found a gun in the kid's locker.

TOM: I see. I do. Certainly. Yes. I can certainly understand your concern, yes. Finding a gun in my son's locker is very disturbing. I agree. It could be worse, but I agree. *(Beat.)* How could it be worse? You're asking me how, specifically, it could be worse? Well, he could've walked into the school cafeteria and started shooting. That would be worse. That would be much worse, don't you agree? Or. He could've waltzed into *your* office, and popped any number of people. That would be worse, too. *(Beat.)* No, I assure you, I am not making light of this situation, believe you me. *(Beat.)* Yes, it is registered in my name. *(Beat.)* Because I work in a funky neighborhood. It's a little bit on the funky side, yes. The *west* side, yes. You know the area. *(Beat.)* I'm in sales. Kovachy Motors. *(Pause.)* *Billy* Kovachy, that's right. *(Beat.)* You know Billy? You do? *(Beat.)* You must have purchased a *car* from us sometimes in the past — is that it? *(Beat.)* I see. And were you *satisfied* with your purchase? *(Beat.)* Let me tell you, that will make him so happy. Billy loves it when a customer drives home satisfied. I will. I'll be sure and tell him. *(Beat.)* No, I do not see any reason to bring the police into this situation. Do you? *(Beat.)* Good. *(Beat.)* This won't happen again. Let me assure you of that. I will see to it personally. *(Beat.)* Yeah, he's a pretty good kid, he's just got all those, what-do-you-call-them, hormones raging through his system. Don't I know it. *(Beat.)* I'll stop by this afternoon and pick it up on my way to work. *(Beat.)* It's been a pleasure talking to *you.*

JULIA
Virginia Coates

Dramatic

> *This is a play about two men in a maternity ward waiting room. One expectant father is talking to another. He doesn't know that the man has just learned that his child has died.*

FATHER TWO: Oh man. I had to get away. Thank God a quiet place. *(No response from Father One.)* Has yours already arrived? Looks like it, since you took off the gown. They sure as hell won't let you in that room without it. Makes you wonder what they think you could give them. I mean, how do they think the kid got here. That wasn't too sterile. Right? *(No response.)* Hey, you OK? You're not going to get sick or faint, are you? . . .

Ya, I know what you mean. All that rushing around. And the yelling, by my wife, that is. She swore she was going to be calm through the whole thing. "I can handle it." She wasn't going to take any drugs. After that first contraction, they couldn't give it to her fast enough. They just gave her Demerol. That's why I could leave. I wish I could drug her up like that all the time. Wish there was time to run down for a cigarette. Told her I was just gonna run out to give an update to the family. *(Pause.)* I feel really bad for the wives though, you know? I thought mine was going to squeeze my hand off. Had to get away from it all, you know? The wife screaming, having to go give updates every fifteen minutes. I think my entire family and neighborhood is out in the waiting room. *(Pause.)* God, all those tubes in her, running every which way. It's weird to see her like that. You know what I mean? *(Pause.)* I guess you can tell this is our first, right? I've never been so nervous about nothin' in my life. How about you, this your first?

LAPIS BLUE, BLOOD RED
Cathy Caplan

Dramatic

> *This "historical drama" about the life and career of the great Renais-*
> *sance painter Artemisia Gentilleschi, is, as you can see by this monologue,*
> *written in a very contemporary style. The play takes place in two time*
> *periods. In one, Artemisia is in her teens and is learning how to paint*
> *from her father, Orazio. In the other, she is a mature woman and is suc-*
> *cessful in her own right. Here, her father (forty-five) has just realized*
> *that she has been having sex with a young acolyte of his.*

ORAZIO: No, we won't eat.

> *(In Tuzia's voice.)* Why doesn't everyone sit down?
>
> *(In his own voice.)* Or why doesn't everyone line up against the
> wall. And I can hit you one after the other. No. I'm not going to eat
> your food. I'm going to eat you. How do you like that? I am run-
> ning three miles each way back and forth twelve times a day between
> this house and up that mountain — hill — chaos — making sure
> you have fresh pigment, making sure you have work, making sure you
> have someone to model for you, making sure the twelve idiots who
> work for me keep painting even when I am out of the room for one
> second. Everyone says your problem Orazio is you're taking on too
> many jobs, taking care of too many people, too much meat on the
> fire. But I say, oh I have my safety net. If I fall off the scaffolding,
> that's bad. But, if I fall off a scaffold and I've got someone to catch
> me, or a rope to catch on to, I'm doing all right. If I have an up-
> stairs tenant who happens to be a pretty close friend of mine, who
> happens to not pay a penny in rent, who assures me, that while I
> am at work, I can leave the worries of my household behind me, that
> she will watch my daughter like a hawk, take care of my baby boy
> like a mother, that is my rope. That is my safety net. I'll worry about
> your daughter. I am forty-five years old. You are thirty-three years

old and you are fucking my daughter who is sixteen years old. Under my roof, in my studio. And what chance do I have of marrying her off now. That makes me mad. Very mad. I'll destroy you. You will never get near this house again. You will never get into the academy. You will never work in Rome. You will never touch her again. I promise you that. Let me build a cross and I'll nail all three of you to it. And when you're finished you can hang me on it too. And then you can come to my funeral ten minutes later. And you will not get one more shred of her and not one more shred of this either. *(Orazio picks up the money.)* Not one more shred of her.

LIMONADE TOUS LES JOURS
Charles L. Mee

Dramatic

> *Andrew is a middle-aged American man in Paris who almost inadvertently begins a romance with a much younger cabaret singer named Jacqueline. Here he is talking with her about the choices he has made in his life in an effort to make some sense of them.*

ANDREW: I married a person because I fell in love
    but I don't know with whom or what.
    She was very beautiful and smart and quirky
    and she seemed stable
    not a crazy person
    because I had had some hot romances before
    but with women who were crazy
    because I like a passionate person . . .
    and it turned out I was always falling in love with crazy people who
    would fly off the handle and curse and scream and throw things . . .
    and, of course, sometimes it must have been my fault
    because, partly, I was cool and rational
    in a way that would drive any normal person crazy . . .
    but also I think I chose people who were erratic and unpredictable
    because I was so rational
    and I wanted someone who would take a sudden turn
    you know and take me to some surprising place
    and then only later did I realize that people who did that
    are often crazy people . . .
    they take these unexpected turns all the time . . .
    and you don't always appreciate it
    you wake up in the morning
    and find a note on the pillow saying
    "I'm going to see Ulu, going to see Ulu,

going to see Ulu Skrebenski"
and you don't know whether it's a poem of a kind
or she is just feeling light-hearted
or she is already drinking at seven o'clock in the morning

and then when we stayed in a hotel
and she ripped up the pillow cases so we could take turns
tying one another to the bedposts

and she had her period so she made sure she got blood on her fingers
and reached back up behind the headboard of the bed
and streaked the wall with blood

or sometimes when she was just happy
she would throw dishes
dish after dish against the wall
just because she felt a little bit happy. . . .
So when I found a stable person at last who was also sexy
I thought: OK, at last, I've found a person I can marry
and that was the fatal thought, I think,
"I've found a person"
which is to say, I'd found a kind of person
a category of person I felt good with . . .
not always sitting on the edge of my chair
wondering what might happen next
someone I could just feel
OK, this is going to be a quiet evening at home
and so I married her . . .
and it's still not clear to me if my mistake was thinking categorically
or, on the other hand,
if the mistake was just that the category was wrong:
stability . . .
or if the mistake was just thinking at all
instead of following my instincts
because I think sometimes I think too much
and not always very clearly or intelligently

and I'd be better off just to say:
oh, right, good, okay, hot, go for it . . .
and live life moment to moment
without thinking about the consequences
weighing and balancing
trying to use a lot of forethought
because that kind of thing always puts you living in the future
which we can't predict
and know nothing about
and simultaneously takes us out of the present
where we are living
and might know something about it if we only paid attention.

So, as you can see,
I don't think I'm a person
who ought to be getting involved with anyone else either.

LIMONADE TOUS LES JOURS
Charles L. Mee

Dramatic

> *Andrew is a middle-aged American man in Paris who almost inadver-*
> *tently begins a romance with a much younger cabaret singer named*
> *Jacqueline. Here he is talking with her about the choices he has made*
> *in his life in an effort to make some sense of them.*

ANDREW: It seems to me
    the trouble always begins with love.
    People always say the trouble is differentness
    or even hatred or prejudice
    or some such bad thing that is the root of all troubles
    but really it's love that always disrupts everything.

    Once you've set love loose in the world
    anything can happen
    if human beings are given free rein to love and, if they don't, you
    can hardly call it love — . . .
    And love pays no attention to what is useful or considerate
    then we throw the world into turmoil with every breath we take
    not just love of another person
    but love of the earth
    love of trees
    love of the country
    of little green farms
    and fenced-off tracts of wild quince with great pink flowers
    the blue air chill but full of the new and subtle warmth of spring . . .
    All these things we cherish and covet
    and protect from the intrusions of others
    love of one's own country
    of one's own friends

of the familiar ways our friends have
their manners and the way that they are dressed
and then
love of wine . . .
love of pleasure
of a picnic in the woods
and sweet red peppers with a pinch of thyme
love of music
love of riches, of speed, of power
all the things that we desire
and even love of sorrow
love of tears
love of heartache
love of anguish
love of exhaustion of sleep of solace
love of warmth, love of pain
love of lasting longer than we think we can
love of loud noises and cheering
of marching steps
of martial music
of causing death

with all these kinds of love
what need is there of hatred?

Hatred is just the kerosene put on the fire.

This must be why there's nothing to be done about it.
You cannot eradicate the human heart itself.

Because it's not the worst in us that leads us into trouble it's the best.

LOOKING FOR NORMAL
Jane Anderson

Seriocomic

Reverend Muncie (could be any age) is visited by Roy, who has come to him for advice. Little does he know (until just after this platitudinous monologue) that Roy's problem is that he believes himself to be a woman mistakenly born into a man's body.

REVEREND MUNCIE: Okay. Roy, do you know how many husbands come in here thinking they're the only one? Good grief, I thought the same thing about myself until I started doing marriage counseling and heard all these complaints from other men. Look, the fact is, long-time married couples are gonna lose some of their passion for each other. And the shame of it is, we start putting the blame on ourselves. Or on the marriage. We think, oh, my wife is indifferent to my urges or gee, she's looking a little frayed around the edges. And you start looking somewhere else for fulfillment. In my case — and I'm not talking out of school because my wife and I have discussed this — there was a time when I started to have feelings for another woman. I knew I'd never act on these feelings but, oh boy, they were there all the time. I was appalled with myself. I thought I was unworthy of my calling, that I should turn in my collar and become a shoe salesman. Then one day, thank goodness, I got this letter from a colleague. He sent me an article he had found on the conflict between our spiritual and our animal selves — I have it here somewhere, I'll make a copy of it for you. But basically it says that God designed the female of a species to be the nester and for the male to travel from herd to herd and impregnate as many females as he could. Then as humans evolved out of the animal world and became civilized, we developed rules about marriage and procreation which made it inappropriate for the male to have many different partners. And that's the conundrum of being a human male. You can love your wife dearly but you still might glance at a pretty woman when you pass her on the street. We can't let these desires get out of hand but on the same token, we can't berate ourselves for having a vestigial urge to roam. . . . I think men, more than women, are still very influenced by the animal side. But I also think that there are also many enlightened parts to being a man — look at the strength of David, the wisdom of Solomon, the patience of Job, the compassion of Jesus.

LOOKING FOR NORMAL
Jane Anderson

Seriocomic

Wayne, a young man (twenties to thirties), has received a most disturbing letter from his father, which he shares with us. Turns out, Pop is going to have a sex-change operation.

WAYNE: *(To audience.)* I just got this letter from my dad. What it says — man, this is . . . I'm fucking speechless. It's not just the content, it's the whole style, it's the — let me just reads it. *(Reading letter.)* "Dear Wayne, I am writing to you at a frightening and also a very exciting crossroads in my life." *(To audience.)* The man who wrote this letter, this man, my pop, is from the corn belt. Self-expression, communication — it's not part of his wiring, okay? He's incapable of talking on the phone without a conversational cue sheet: Hello Wayne, how's your van, the clutch still jamming? Have you gotten that health insurance like I told you? What's the name of the band you're working for? Nope, never heard of them. Well, I'm gonna give you back to your mother, now And then Mom gets on to fill in the blanks — your father misses you, Wayne, but he's happy that you called and he loves you very much. And now I'm reading this letter, wondering if this is maybe some bizarre joke someone's playing on me, but no, I know for a fact that this is from Pop because he's the only one I know who would write a personal letter on his business stationery. Dad, come on, we all know you're cheap, but if you're going to drop this kind of shit on me — okay, let's go on. *(Reading letter.)* "I think that you, more than anyone else in our family, will understand what I need to do. You have always been a rebel. Since you were a little boy, you always insisted on marching to your own drumbeat. Although I got mad at you for some of the things you did, I always secretly admired your spunk and your wonderful free spirit." *(To audience.)* I used to do trick-riding on my granddad's

49

tractor. One time I fell off and it kept going and almost ran over my head. Gramps strapped the bejusus out of me, but Pop — Pop just held on to me and cried. *(Reading.)* "I don't know how to break this news to you, other than in a letter. I'm going to have surgery next year to correct a condition I have that is known as gender dysphoria. In other words I am a woman born in a man's body and I will be getting a sex change." *(To audience.)* Let me read that to you again. "I am a woman born in a man's body and I will be getting a sex change." Let's go on. "Your mother and I are still trying to decide what to do about our living arrangements. She needs some time to adjust to this new situation" — no shit. And let's see, oh he's starting electrolysis and hormone treatments in two weeks and by November he'll be "more feminine in appearance" — excellent, Pop, just in time for the holidays. And I like this part, "I haven't told your sister yet but when I do, I'd like you to give her a call and see how she's doing" — sure, no problem. Hey Sis, how's tricks? Moving on. "I know it will take time for you to understand and accept what I'm doing. I've tried to be a good father to you while you were growing up. You're now a grown man who's out on his own and you don't need me anymore to set an example. I hope you understand that I'd like to find some peace and happiness in my life. I still am your parent no matter what and will care deeply about you until the end of my days. I love you, Dad." *(A beat.)* Let me read that part again: "I love you, Dad." One more time: "I love you, Dad." What do I do with this? Someone please tell me, what do I do with this? *(Blackout.)*

MIDNIGHT IN THE MARIGNY
Barret O'Brien

Comic

Pappy (thirties to forties) is head of a group of nuts who are trying to fight back against the Starbucks-ization of America.

PAPPY: Listen . . . "Starbucks plans to open one-thousand stores outside of North America by 2003 . . ." It's today's colonialism. Like Britain was to India, or Ghengis Khan to Asia, these multi-international corporations are to us. These tyrannical monsters moving from town to town destroying culture and practices. Transferring profits to some far-off land and reducing the local inhabitants to indentured servants, minimum-wage counter workers in baseball caps and a smock. And here we've held out, New Orleans has held out for a long time. Hidden down here among the swamps we've clutched on to our heritage with both hands. But we're breaking. *(He takes out the map and points to different areas.)* The first Starbucks was opened uptown next door to Coffee and Company in 1998 and within six months Coffee and Company went out of business. Next they open across the street from Café Luna on Magazine Street, it's faltering. Another store on Magazine one block from PJ's, one on Veteran's Highway with a drive-through! A drive-through! Earlier this year they opened one on Decatur St. in the French Quarter and within the year Kaldi's, the most pure coffee establishment in the city, closes its doors for the last time. Kaldi's was a haven for freaks . . . and artists . . . and poets . . . and dreamers. I used to play chess with a guy named Earl there back when they were open twenty-four hours. He had these deep-set gray eyes and we used to play in absolute silence till the sun rose. It made me feel alive. Like part of a great poem. Like how I feel here. In the Marigny. Where I step out my door and feel part of something. Like I belong. One of the few places in this washed-out excuse for a country that actually feels like somewhere. Different. Apart. And now

Starbucks is attempting to come here. The Marigny is possibly the most preserved part of the entire city and you want to just allow them to just roll on in unencumbered? To transfer what little money we have in this part of the city from Ed at Café Flora to this 1.47 billion-dollar-a-year monster in Seattle, Washington. No. We have an opportunity here. . . .

To say something. Every day we lose another part of this city. Every day its another Walgreens, another Texaco, another Burger King popping up like pimples on the landscape. . . .

And we accept it passively. Well, I won't. I won't sit back while my culture is erased. . . . So that the only memory my children have of this city is a faded black-and-white photograph of a town that no longer exists. *(Lays a hand on the banner.)* This is our Boston Tea Party. And, no, it's not the most genius plan ever devised, but it's something. A pronouncement that we will not be bought and sold for the price of a vanilla latte. Not us. Not in this part of the world.

MIDNIGHT IN THE MARIGNY
Barret O'Brien

Comic

> *Pappy (thirties to forties) is head of a group of nuts who are trying to fight back against the Starbucks-ization of America.*

PAPPY: I hate shit. I'm so sick of shit, Ken. That son of a bitch . . . Who was that girl? The night manager? My mother sits at home patiently while he pokes teenage girls after hours in his . . .

   . . . he wasn't always like this, you know? He was an idealist. Got kicked out of Fortier for refusing to say the pledge of allegiance. He went to Woodstock, for Christ sake. And now he's executive manager of all southeastern Starbuck franchises. How does that happen? What makes a man give up everything he believes in for stock options and a sports utility vehicle? I mean, is that what's going to happen to us? I'm so sick. Of money, and society, and my father, of this crippled country we've been handed. Full of prepackaged foodstuffs and bad TV and starless skies. It's like everything's getting bigger and brighter and if it continues soon it'll just be this immense neon balloon of commerce and industry hovering above the city, eclipsing the sun, bursting into the windows of our houses. We'll just be sitting here in our La-Z-Boys watching syndicates of *Full House* hooked to a intravenous McDonald's feed while these goddam international mega-corporate conglomerations pump Cheetos and Pepsi and one hundred free hours of America Online into our veins! We'll be born, we'll purchase, and we'll die.

MUERTE EN LA MENTE
Raul H. Castillo

Dramatic

> *The title of this play means, in English, "Death on My Mind." It takes*
> *place in an old abandoned shack in the desert. In this monologue, which*
> *begins the play, Marco, a middle-aged Mexican-American man, is talk-*
> *ing to Joaquin, who is younger. They are smugglers of "illegal aliens"*
> *across the border from Mexico to the United States.*

MARCO: Goddamn, I never been so hot in my life; it's like walking in a
fucking frying pan! Must be one fifteen, ONE TWENTY easily. *Chi-*
nagado . . . that's ridiculous! I thought we would never find shade.
When we first saw this place, I thought it was a mirage . . . couldn't
believe it, *estaba todo aguitado. (Looks around.)* Man, who the hell
would live out here? Guy must be crazy. A little *locito*, man, the *Tejas*
desert is no place for someone to be stranded in. This place will eat
you alive, man, swallow you up! *Puta madre*, I can't believe this! *Chin-*
gos of cars on the highway, and I just happen to be in the one that
this *pendejo* . . . COP, decides to pull over. *Porque, porque yo?* Man,
that's bad luck. Plain bad luck. Why does that shit always happen
to me? Always me! There's a million other *pendejos* out there who
deserve it more than I do! NAW, but it's me that always ends up the
loser. Why? That's what I want to know! *(Beat.)* And you know . . .
you know what? Nothing would have happened if that idiot with
the *vaquero* hat wouldn't have gotten sick in Falfurias. That put us
back half an hour. I bet you we would have been through that exact
same spot thirty minutes earlier, that pig would have been at Dunkin'
Donuts or something. Just not there. I wouldn't have to deal with
these *pendejadas. (Beat.)* And that stupid old lady with the little girl.
Didn't I tell them to urinate before we left? Didn't I? See, that's what
I get for being such a good guy. People take advantage of good guys.
I should have just said no. Let them suffer. I don't care. Any other

driver would have said no. But me, I'm a nice guy. And what do I get for being a nice guy? I get dicked. Shit! Bad luck. *(Beat.)* Whatever . . . we're somewhere, huh? It's good to be out of that sun, man. I thought I would be cooked alive. Lady on the radio said today was supposed to be the hottest day of the year. *(Beat.)* The hottest day of the year! Can you believe that? *(Beat.)* See, it makes sense. If this was going to happen to me, it had to be on the hottest day of the year. If I was going to be walking around the Texas desert aimlessly for who-the-hell-knows-how-many hours, it had to be on the hottest day of the year. It couldn't happen any other way, because that wouldn't fit into what has come to be known as my life. *El Colmo, es el colmo!* I should have listened to my father and become a priest. That's what I should have done.

THE MYSTERY OF ATTRACTION
Marlane Meyer

Dramatic

Warren (twenties to thirties) is in trouble for having taken nude photographs of a fourteen-year-old girl. Here he is telling his side of the story to his brother Ray.

WARREN: You don't know these girls nowadays, man, they grow up fast what with MTV and all kinds of sexy talk in the school yard and these movies, all kinds of movies about sex and longing and the unfulfilled promise of love, and they can't say NO, they don't have language, the schools don't encourage debate so you can do what you like as long as YOU keep talking and it doesn't hurt them and you know they all want to be models so they can be wanted by millions of lonely men humping their mattresses in the middle of the night, jerking off to these images in their heads while their wives make up stories about how THEY can't have sex tonight. Bleeding, gas, imaginary pains, and if YOU complain it's always about what's wrong with YOU. I'm selfish because I wake her up when the bed starts shaking because I have to relieve myself manually, and she is disgusted and starts screaming and it makes you want to kill these women when they lose their love for you and all they want to do is use you for a paycheck and complain to their friends about what kind of animal in heat you've turned out to be and how it's all gotten worse as you've gotten older and uglier and all the time they're keeping this precious thing you need so deep inside themselves, so hidden, they keep it deep inside where you need to be, but they won't let you back in there, they can't let you in because of something that happened, you don't know what it is, it's a mystery, they won't talk to you about it and you ask them what's wrong and they say nothing, nothing, nothing and meanwhile you're dying of loneliness because it's lonely out here.

THE MYSTERY OF ATTRACTION

Marlane Meyer

Dramatic

Larry is a vicious loan-shark enforcer known as "Bone Daddy," so called because he takes bones from his victims who have refused to pay up. Here, he shows up late at night, interrupting a conversation between two brothers, one of whom owes a loan shark a lot of money.

LARRY: Hi, Ray. What're you doin'? Havin' a party? A boy party? . . . Warren, Larry . . . glad to meet you. So you're Ray's brother. *(Beat, looks around, to Ray.)* That's nice. To have a brother. How you doin', Ray? . . .

That's not what I hear. I hear you suck. . . .

No, stay here. You stay where you are, *(To Ray.)* don't you love that, the respect of men for other men's privacy, that is so important, women never understand that, do they? They are too curious. Not that I'm not a curious person. But mostly about real things. Three-dimensional objects as opposed to feelings. I don't really have feelings but I do have hobbies. . . .

I study anatomy. It's a most useful science in my line of work. To know exactly how to separate a joint, pop, where to apply the pressure, crack, where to make an incision. *(Sound.)* The mess you can avoid with a little education. . . .

(Larry pulls a collarbone out of his pocket.) Ever see one of these? . . .

It's a clavicle or collarbone of a sixty-four-year-old used car salesman in Vegas, washed up on his luck. The trick is to take the bone while the guy is awake. They scream like babies these old men, you wouldn't believe it. Then they pass out and wake up, this area around the chest is all caved in . . . it's just impossible to imagine the pain and you can't move without screaming in agony and then they put this prosthetic piece in there that never sits right. There's a clicking sound every time you take a breath just so you never forget what a loser you are. *(Larry moves to the door.)* However. This is not your fate. Clavicle. No sir. Our mutual acquaintances have instructed me to prepare a very special treat for you. So. I'll be seein' you Ray. Not now, but soon. By the light of the moon. *(Howls.) (Larry exits.)*

THE MYSTERY OF ATTRACTION

Marlane Meyer

Dramatic

Warren (twenties to thirties) is talking to his brother Ray about the woman they both loved, named Sharky.

WARREN: When Sharky came home and started to scream I struck her not in anger so much as surprise. And she fell into the glass door and thrashing to keep from falling ended up cutting herself even worse, in fact, she punctured an artery. . . .

She was asking me to help but I couldn't . . . I saw what was happening, but I couldn't seem to consider it an emergency. How could I? It was a triumph. I was finally on level ground. She was so weak and pathetic that all my hatred came out and I remained absolutely motionless and watched her dying. Her screaming turned to begging and the begging turned to crying till finally . . . and this is how I found out she still loved you . . . when she realized she was going to die, she asked me to tell you that she had always loved you, that there was never anyone else in her heart. And then, she apologized to me, she did . . . *(Smiles.)* She apologized which I must admit, felt good. That broke the spell, the apology. When she did that I tried to help her, but by then it was too late. She was gone. . . .

She told me she wasn't trying to fix me, she was trying to make me more like you. Isn't that sweet?

(Moves to the garden.) I put her out there. Out there under the Plumeria and the gardenia, where the jasmine is in bloom, where the garden smells the sweetest. I put her out there for you. Deep in the rich fragrant earth. She'll be mother to your garden, nurturing it for years to come, if you leave her alone. Can you do that, Ray? Can you let her rest in peace?

NAVY WIFE
Jason Milligan

Dramatic

> Navy Wife *is a play about a military couple who live on a base. Jack is a navy flier, gone for months at a time. His wife, Claire, to whom he is speaking, knows her marriage is in trouble. Here, Jack is talking to her about why he is so unhappy.*

JACK: I don't know what to say to you anymore, Claire. I don't . . . Nothing seems to work when I'm home, not like it used to. Nothing . . . *(He's really honest with this, totally earnest. He really wants her to understand:)* The only time I'm really alive . . . is when I'm up there. *(Beat.)* Just one sheet of glass between me and the whole sky and I'm up there, in the center of it all, blue all around me, blue in front of me, and I'm streaking through it so fast you can't hold me back. That's what it is, Claire, I've never tried to explain it to you before but it's the feeling — I'm up there and I'm in control and I'm miles above everything and I know nothing or no one can hold me back. Those are the moments I feel most alive. Those are the moments when — . But, you have to come back down. Sooner or later, you're back on the deck and you've lost some of that thrill and then you're drinking with the rest of the guys and you've lost even more of the thrill and then you're coming home and it — it's just gone. Sometimes that thrill feels like . . . all there is, and you wonder why you come home, and — *(He looks at her, sees he's not communicating.)* I'm lost, Claire. I'm just really . . . lost. And I don't know how to find my way back home.

NAVY WIFE
Jason Milligan

Dramatic

> *Navy Wife is a play about a military couple who live on a base. Jack is a navy flier, gone for months at a time. His wife, Claire, to whom he is speaking, knows her marriage is in trouble. Here, Jack is talking to her about why he is so unhappy.*

JACK: Claire! Quit *helping* me!! You follow me around like some dog, don't you know how that makes me feel? . . .

    The guilt, Claire! The — will you look around? Look at this place! It's a piece of junk! I keep trying to convince myself, "yeah, I could come back and live here," but I can't live here, Claire. No more than I can live in the sky! I look around and I see what a junk heap this is. And it's always gonna be a junk heap, no matter what you do to it! I don't care if you put up lace curtains or cook me breakfast or hem every pair of pants I own! None of that makes this feel like home, Claire. It just makes me feel *guilty! (Pause.)* I have *tasted* something, Claire. You gotta understand. Tasted something that I can't come down from! I keep trying to find some — some *place* I fit in, somewhere in between the sky and the ground, somewhere in between heaven and hell, somewhere in between my plane and this pit! I've been trying to convince myself that this is my home, but it doesn't work anymore. Every time I come back here and see this dinky little place and see you trying to make it livable . . . it makes me gag. It chokes me, Claire. It rises up in my throat like vomit and chokes me. We have nothing in this whole world that we share except this horrible, dingy, dirty little apartment and four square feet of yard! . . .

    They *lied* to us, Claire! . . . All those promises were lies! Look around, Claire! This is as good as it gets! This is our life! This is the best we can do and it stinks!

    (Long pause. Jack stands there, breathing hard.)

I dunno what happened, Claire. It's like I really do live two lives . . . one here and one Out There. You said it yourself: I'm away most of the time and the truth is, I like being Out There more than I like being here. I keep trying to come "home" to you . . . but I don't know if I want to come home anymore.

NOVEMBER
Don Nigro

Seriocomic

Rooks, a determined man in his twenties to thirties, is intent on getting his elderly aunt to sign over her land to him, so he can "develop" it.

ROOKS: I'm nice. When wasn't I nice? Listen, we're gonna make you proud, Aunt Liz, we're gonna make you rich off that land of yours. We're gonna put grasshoppers on it to pump out the oil, strip-mine the hill and get all that coal under there, the gas company's gonna pump out all the gas, and we still got all that room out by the barn for me to start my auto salvage business. That place is gonna produce, Lizzy. You been sittin on top of a gold mine all these years and didn't even know it. We're gonna make lots of money, and I'm gonna be important for a change. People are gonna respect me, and you won' never have to worry about nothing again, I swear. And Becky and me can go to Las Vegas and Atlantic City and all them classy places, and she'll be happy. I'll make her happy, and you'll be happy because Becky's happy and everybody will be happy, okay? . . .

    Okay. Great. GREAT. I'll be good to you from now on, I promise. I ain't such a bad guy when you get to know me, honest I'm not. I got to go tell everybody at the Cootie Club. I never been so happy in my whole life. See you later, nurse.

OTHER PEOPLE
Christopher Shinn

Comic

Stephen, a gay man in his twenties, is having dinner with his ex-boyfriend and his current roommate, a poet and stripper named Petra. Stephen is a playwright and Web-site movie critic.

STEPHEN: Because, no, listen: When you guys were away, endless misery for the first six months, incessant, but this one night, like less than two months ago, I had this epiphany, this total — Can we even get some bread while we're — Mark, do you want any bread? I'll get the waiter. *(As Stephen looks around, signals.)* . . .

Anyway so, this guy. The date. Café, nice, blah blah, we swap stories, walk around the East Village, blab about ex-boyfriends, look at some clothes, decide, what the hell, let's go see a show! So we go to the half-price booth, we go to this musical, musical's over, so we go — Darren — *Darren's* his name — so the show lets out, we go for a drink. Now this will sound banal, mundane, but — we're in the bar — and I start to tell Darren about this *grant* I'm applying for for this *play* I've written — and by the way I'm nervous because I should be hearing if I got this grant or not before the new year, so keep your eye out in the mail — anyway — I tell him how I had just gotten so frustrated with my *job* and how I'd stopped even going on *auditions* because the stuff I was sent out for was so *wretched* and so how I decided to write a *play* — you know, and when you guys left I went back into therapy — and I'm just beginning to really *figure out* my patterns, you know, just, *pathological* sex and and this really degraded self-loathing "love" instinct I mean not-love but — but — I'm lonely, you know? You guys are — I'm kind of hating my life still and — I'm really *hot* for this guy actually, I mean he's *totally* — he has this weirdo pseudo-British accent sort of, he's a musician, he's got this really sexy, like, *detachment* going on, this really careless *swagger* and *ambivalence* — . . .

Okay, okay: So I tell him about the grant and the play and he says he wants to read it. "I'd really like to read it, Stephen. Sounds totally cool." But I feel — I feel *weird*. I feel *something's off here*. Because — and I realize — I turn around briefly because I realize something about his *gaze* — he's not quite looking at me, he's sort of just looking *above* me, above my shoulder, and he's been fixed there the whole — and so I look behind me and I see that — and my heart — *breaks* — I see that he's watching the TV — above the bar. As he's talking to me. The — so I say, "Derek? Derek?" And he says, "Hold on." . . .

He, whatever — "Hold on." And it's not — the show is like *Entertainment Tonight* but not, it's like a *lighter* version of *Entertainment Tonight*, they're interviewing some *blonde* woman, some *sitcom,* and I turn back around and I start to say something else you know and he says, "One more sec." *One more sec.* And. And so. I mean that's it. . . .

NO! No he asked me to go home with him and I just said — "Not tonight but I'll call" or whatever. Because, you know, because I *saw* at that moment — I understood — I thought: *How many of the people I've slept with have actually looked at me?* And I decided no, I decided, I will not go to bed with *anyone* for the rest of my *life* whom I do not perceive has at the very least an *interest in me as a human being*. You know, as a separate person. Because — you know? There I am, sitting before him, a real — TV — me — and he picks — because *no.* Because that will not be my life. Anymore.

OTHER PEOPLE
Christopher Shinn

Comic

Stephen, a struggling playwright and Web-site movie critic in his twenties, has invited his ex-boyfriend Mark to spend Christmas with him. Here, he is talking to Mark.

STEPHEN: They did not like, listen to this, they did not like my *blurbs,* my blurbs were *rejected,* two of the four because, they said, they used words like *brisk* and *self-assured* as being qualities my blurbs did not *have,* you know, meaning, these are not *arch* enough — straight-faced, I'm sitting in the office, I'm nervous actually nervous, and, and have you noticed this trend among women, this trend where they do not *like* homosexual men, I mean I know that's a dangerous generality but she said, These are too *soft,* these lack *punch,* I mean, she might as well have said I don't have the *balls* to write a blurb of *Men in Black.* So. So now I have to rewrite the blurbs and it's like, look, I don't want to go back to temping, which was which was *soul-murder,* which was pure degradation every hour on the hour, and I don't certainly do not want to "bartend" again and it's getting to the point where it's like — I mean I'm not gonna *move* where would I *move* Los Angeles? And it's — but what, can I do to make more money that will not take all my energy and slowly and utterly *kill* me because I have been there before, you know, Huck Finn, "I've been there before," and, you know, he's off floating on a raft and happy and won't be civilized and of course he won't go back, he's a bright guy, but then, you know, Mark Twain wrote the book, not Huck Finn — *(Apartment buzzer.)* Well. Saved by the buzzer just as I was getting coherent. But I am, I'm enraged, and am I *wrong,* you know, am I *indulgent,* well I say *No* because that's what they want me to think so I'll shut up and be a good little — *(Pushing intercom button.)* Hello?

PROFESSIONAL SKEPTICISM
James Rasheed

Dramatic

> *Paul (thirties) works for a top accounting firm. Here he is talking to another accountant about ethics issues. Pretty timely, huh?*

PAUL: I've been thinking a lot lately about professional skepticism. . . .
Greg, I'm talking to you. Please sit down. *(Pause.)* . . .

Good, I got your attention. Let's talk about professional skepticism. You're Greg, the auditor and I'm Paul, the client. We become good buddies. Best buds. You're auditing my books and you find discrepancies. But you think to yourself, Paul's my good friend. Best bud. Your judgment is clouded. You've lost your professional skepticism. This whole time, Paul, the client, is thinking of new ways to screw you. *(Pause.)* I just thought of another example. Look at us. Our company operates under a pyramidal structure. At the bottom of the pyramid are the staff accountants, like you and me. As you move up you have the seniors, then the managers and finally the partners. At each level there are fewer and fewer. But we all want to be on top. Yet there are very few tops and a lot of bottoms. My question is, should we be friends with one another? Let down our guard? . . .

(Looking directly at Greg.) You told Pam you had found my weaknesses and you were trying to make my life miserable. . . .

Leo, please let me finish. It's important to me. Thank you. There are those who believe that to succeed they must destroy other people. They better be careful they don't destroy themselves. *(Pause.)* Back to auditing!

SORROWS AND REJOICINGS
Athol Fugard

Dramatic

> *Dawid is essentially a ghost, or memory, of a recently deceased South African poet in his fifties. This monologue is a memory of what he said to Marta, his black housekeeper and lover, years before.*

DAWID: *(Passionate and intensely alive, a sheet of paper in his hand.)* Listen to this!

(He plays with the names, exploring and enjoying them for their rich musicality:)

Appolis, Arries, April

Baartman, Baadjies, Bokbaard and Bruintjies

Carelse

Duimpies

Goliath and Grootboom

January, Japhta, Julies and Jantjies

Kleinbooi

Malgas, Muggles and Meintjies

November

Plaatjies, Persensie

Sambok, September, Stuurman

Vaaltyn, Voetpad, Vetbooi

Witbooi . . .

Yes of course, names, and straight from a Karoo telephone directory. What's so wonderful about them? Come on, Marta! Take a couple and roll them around in your mouth and taste them . . . *(He demonstrates.)* Jantjies . . . Jantjies . . . Jantjies and Bruintjies . . . Jantjies, Bruintjies and Duimpies . . . *(He smacks his lips.)* They taste of the Karoo . . . sweet water and dry dust!

Close your eyes and play with "Arries" long enough and you'll hear that little whisper of relief when a little breeze stirs the leaves of the old bluegum tree at the end of a hot day. Do the same with "Vaaltyn" and you'll see the Karoo veld in the middle of a drought, gray and brittle, and if it's sweetness you want then play with "Marta" and "Barends" . . .

Marta Barends! When I roll that around in my mouth I taste Karoo food, Karoo sweetness. Warm crusty brown bread just out of the oven and honey, wild aloe honey, thorntee honey. Warm Bruin Brood en Doringboom Heuning!

Incredible isn't it . . . a poem . . . an almost perfect little poem and it comes straight from the Karoo telephone directory! One more poem for the collection! I want it to be the first one. And it comes complete with a title: "Karoo Directory."

Hell, Marta! This land of ours. So beautiful! But also so cruel! Sometimes I think old Eugene Marais was right in his "Song of South Africa": She give nothing, but demands everything. Tears, the names of the dead, the widow's lament, the pleading gestures and cries of children . . . all mean nothing to her. She claims as her holy right, the fruits of endless pain.

No! Don't cry. It's only a poem, Marta . . . Marta Barends! . . . Warm brown bread and thorntree honey . . . Yes! You are all of that.

STRANGER
Craig Lucas

Dramatic

Hush (thirties to forties, played by David Strathairn in the original Off-Broadway production) has recently been released from prison for kidnapping a young woman and locking her in a trunk. Here, he is on an airplane, talking to another woman named Linda.

HUSH: . . . When I was fifteen? . . .

    I heard voices telling me things . . . what to do, who to listen to . . . I knew I wasn't supposed to tell anybody . . . that the voices were another world, speaking . . . through me; I'd been selected, and I felt special . . . They said I was God. They said I had created the world, it was, everything, everybody . . . all . . . everybody was pretending that I wasn't who I really was . . . and so I had to say the right things, do the right things . . . .

    Or . . . it would all explode . . . and everything would be destroyed. I could do that, the part of me that knew the truth . . . Their suffering would all have been useless. They were the voices of saints who'd suffered torment — . . . fire, knives arrows, all of the — singing — Even buying a pack of gum, it was important what coins I used, whether they were copper or silver, nickel plate . . . Everything had a symbolism. Which is how the devil works, in symbols. God works through Love — Love alone. But I didn't know that. I thought it was God, I thought it was me talking to me . . . from deep outside and inside. Probably what . . . I don't know, probably what the Pope thinks, that he speaks for God. Or the Ayatollah. That's always the Devil, if you think you speak for God. But I didn't know that. And the voices got louder and, I started flunking out. My parents were really freaked. They were in denial. I was being bad. By the time they threw me out . . . I couldn't hold a reasonable conversation, I was possessed by the voices telling me: Don't look this person in the eye, that is Satan, you are holding everything in balance, the stars, you are the universe itself. I was hospitalized, picked up by the cops and put in a state home, and medicated; they said the urges were me, mine, which I couldn't acknowledge, so I assigned them to "outside" — "others" — that I identified with the martyred saints, and it was my own anger projected onto imaginary — Anyway I was released. My hair fell out. I was living in an abandoned cottage in Coburn, you know where that is? Way out . . . Living off garbage and stolen cans, I would wander around in New Hope after dark, and panhandle. I had this old car. And the voices said . . . to kill a girl. She had to be the right girl. I had to . . . fix myself up, cut my beard, buy a new shirt, cologne, and spruce up, go to a bar, and I would know who she was. God would tell me: she was to be the sacrifice, like the Inca, you know? The ancient people? They would pick a virgin, a little girl, and dope her up, march her up the side of the mountain and bash her skull in. To appease the gods. And it was an honor. And I was the last true voice of the True God. She would join them: the hosts of all the saints, the angels. *(Pause.)* Her name was Diane, she was tall . . . had dark hair, kind of funny features, kinda like a Inca girl, I think . . . And I chatted her up. I could hold it together if I knew there was a reason, a purpose, and I invited her back to my cabin and she came . . . We drove, it's a long long way, and she seemed excited, and not afraid. And we got there. I didn't have electricity, just lamps, and an oil burner, all hippie like, I told her it was an ethical choice, I wasn't stupid. I'm not stupid. . . .

Told her I had to go pee, and when I came out of the bathroom, I . . . and kissed her, and . . . I chained her up. And a voice in me was saying Don't do it, don't do it. And I thought that was the Devil. But I couldn't . . . I couldn't be sure . . . And the voice of God, the voices I thought was God said, Kill her quick. With your teeth, anything. But they were in battle . . . Join her . . . to us, join her to Sebastian and Joan and Saint Catherine. . . . The two . . . And so . . . I thought I'd keep her alive until I could know, for sure, and I . . . put her in a trunk. And kept her there.

TALES FROM THE DAILY TABLOID

Jeanne Murray Walker

Comic

> *This comedy is about a Big City ad man who returns to his hometown with an assignment from a tabloid newspaper to collect stories about all the "weird" people there. One of these is a young man named Leroy, whose thumb has been bleeding for three years. Here, he tells Leonard, the "journalist," his story.*

LEROY: . . . I'm afraid they'll find out I did it since I can't stop the bleeding, but I've got an alibi worked out — I sliced it skinning croaker. If they believe that, they're dumber than I think, 'cause a knife cuts clean and auto glass breaks jagged and gives a ragged cut, which is what I've got. I went to work in Wadena at sixteen, after my old man left. We install glass in cars. It's quiet as a graveyard since we all wear gloves. Not to protect our hands, to protect the glass. Outside, around the parking lot, there's windows lined up between wood stakes — one city block of glass that can catch the sun mornings and shine like water. At first I liked putting windows into cars. Replacing something smashed is better than serving meat that turns to shit in hours. Plus which, I thought I'd get some overtime, enough to buy a keyboard. My old lady said I could keep everything I made over the rent. But bucks go fast and overtime is scarcer than a pretty mama here, so I have to practice on a keyboard I drew on paper and it don't make no sound. What kept getting to me was the quiet, like all those millions of car windows resting on their sides between the stakes was sheet after sheet of frozen sound. I started to hate Manny, the guy who brought them in. I'd see him unloading used ones from the truck and I'd want to kill him for saving them from the wrecker, like keeping their music locked inside this thin glossy sheet. So I got a hammer, cut the wire fence, and started smashing. The night I let the music out the sky was all bright riffs and chords and now my head is clear. If only I could do something about this bleeding thumb of mine. Can you hear that music?

THE THEORY OF EVERYTHING
Prince Gomolvilas

Comic

Seven Asian Americans are gathered on top of a Las Vegas wedding chapel for their weekly UFO watch. Here, Nef (twenties) has been asked by a woman named Patty to explain his theory about the Meaning of It All.

NEF: Well, I learned that Albert Einstein wasted the last years of his life searching for The Theory of Everything. He never found it. He failed. . . .

What's the Theory of Everything? It's, um, an all-encompassing paradigm that would explain the entire universe. You know, a unifying formula that would reveal how the universe works. . . .

My very own Theory of Everything is more simple — more philosophical, rather than scientific. . . .

Like I like think of The Theory of Everything as an abstract idea. *My* Theory of Everything is the concept of entropy. It's the complete breakdown of *all* things, living and non-living. I mean, everything that exists in this world, everything comprised of *any* type of matter is being hurled on a one-way irreversible trajectory toward decay and non-existence, and in the case of human beings it's called death. And no one can stop the inevitable, no one can reverse it. Like, like, for example, take a coffee cup, sitting on the edge of a table. If I were to knock that coffee cup onto the ground, it would shatter into pieces. From the moment it's knocked off that table to the moment it hits the ground and shatters, it's acting out The Theory of Everything. Once pushed off the table, there's no going back. Once shattered, it remains shattered. It can't renew itself, can't become whole again. Just like human beings. Once dead, we remain so for eternity. So you see: the moment we were born: We were pushed. Off. The table.

TRANSATLANTIC
Judy Klass

Comic

Bernie Greenfield is a guy from New York who was a Rhodes Scholar years ago. He encountered a lot of American bashing while in England, and now he is revisiting the country for the first time since then. His anger and defiance and defensiveness are back — but so is his buried Anglophilia; deep down, he really wants to impress the British, to somehow get their approval. He is speaking to his wife Lori at their bed and breakfast before going to dinner with Nicholas and Fiona Thorpe, a London couple. Bernie's indie film company wants to produce Fiona's screenplay about Victorian intellectuals. Bernie is afraid Lori will embarrass him; he is wishing that Lori had not come along. He tries to advise and charm and cajole her into behaving the way he wants her to.

BERNIE: Yeah, Lori, listen. Remember what I said, all right? Try not to fawn all over the British, please. It's bad for them, it only encourages them. I mean, don't degrade yourself, sweetheart, for a bunch of limey bastards with poles up their ass. It's not worth it. It's just . . . look. Every time you hear a British accent, you start gushing, and they quietly sneer, and you're so entranced, you don't even notice. I'm not saying be rude. I'm just saying — we're not a colony anymore. There was a big revolution. The sun has set. There's no need to grovel . . . Yes, this trip will be good for us. Lazy afternoons. Long walks. Wild sex. The whole second honeymoon schemer, just like you want. But meanwhile, I need this woman's respect. And little things matter. You're — both of us are loud, exuberant Americans. We've got to tone it down around the Brits. Not be too eager. Hmm? I just want to spare you some soggy British contempt. Look, Lori, believe me, I swear I used to be just like you. Raised in a house full of raving Anglophile Jews. I was weaned on PBS, you know? Same as you. And then I came over here . . . I appreciate British literature.

I admire their command of irony and understatement, and the high level of discourse on their TV. They have good cheap theater — we should catch some this week. They have funny alternative comedians, or used to. The British make better beer than we do, and woollier sweaters. I like this country. It's just the people I could do without.

UNLEASHED
John Godber

Dramatic

> *Mick, an ex-art student in his twenties, is a janitor at a sex club in the red-light district in Amsterdam. He's British (Yorkshire); but for your purposes he could be any nationality — even American.*

> *Mick is standing center. He takes up the mop and begins to mop the stage once again as we saw at the beginning of the play. He mops vigorously.*

MICK: I never tell anybody what I do. Like it's not on my passport, do you know what I mean? I think we're very constipated when it comes to sex. They're very casual about it out here. It's right in your face out here. I tell you, I've seen that many porno films in this last year, that when I get into a lift with a woman, I expect her to go down on me. No, I do! It must have an effect, do you know what I mean? I mean to say, if you lock it away and pretend it doesn't exist, that's not right, and I don't know whether this is any better, to be honest! *(He mops more.)* And it's all for men, isn't it? I mean, don't get me wrong, but what would it be like if all these windows had men stood in them? Eh? Can you imagine that? All stood there in their little white knickers, with their knobs in a pouch? I bet we wouldn't get as many down here then. Maybe we would. *(He mops more.)* I don't know, but it makes me wonder about men. You see, I think men would actually shag somebody different every day, given half the chance! Most of the blokes I know want to have sex with every woman they meet. "Hallo, how are you? Nice to meet you! Right, knickers off, very nice! What were you going to say, more tea, vicar?" That's the beauty of Amsterdam, you can do that here! Yes, men are pretty pathetic when it comes to women, always have been, always will be, it's a universal given! *(He stops mopping.)* Fucking hell, that's a mega thought, isn't it? What about that, me coming out with a mega

77

thought? *(He puts on his Dennis costume.)* When I saw Dennis stood out here, I was going to talk to him, I was going to have a little chat, but I wasn't sure what to say: I was going to say "All right, then, Dennis, how are you, mate? You won't remember me, but we used to live across the road at number thirty-eight, my mam did your ironing, when your wife had migraine. You looking for a shag, then?" But it's not the sort of thing you say, is it? So I just nodded, and he nodded back like suddenly he was Mr. Sex Show and he knew all about what went off down here . . .

UPRIGHT
James Hilburn

Dramatic

This play is about two small-time drug dealers. Here, Paint, in his early fifties, is talking to Pelf, who is much younger.

PAINT: Shit. OK, I got the scarf a few years back. I was working at this sandwich shop in Oldtown, just cleaning up every once in a while. The guy who owned it ran it himself for about fifty years. He was this tough old World War II bastard. Then one day he decides he's gonna retire and close down the shop. So he gets this idea to sell all of his stock at half price and give away free hot dogs. He gets all the employees together, including me, and we gathered up everything: food, magazines, beer. We marked everything for half price. And people came. They didn't care that this store was closing down. They just wanted stuff for cheap. It was a busy day, and I must have handed out a million hot dogs. After five o'clock, business dies down. People are all going home from work. So me and this guy are sweeping up. The old man is behind the register counting the money we made, when the door busts open and two guys wearing ski masks run in and yell, "Give us the money." The old man yells back, "Fuck you." So one of the robbers shoots the guy I'm working with. I'm thinking that we're all gonna die, but the old man just looks at them real cool and all and says, "Go ahead and kill them, I don't give a shit. Just means I don't have to pay them tomorrow." One of the crooks turns his gun on me, and I just close my eyes. I was pretty sure I was gonna die. Then I hear this loud "Wham," and the old guy starts swearing. When I finally open my eyes, I see a dead robber in front of me and blood everywhere. The old man had pulled out a gun and shot him, but the other one got away. He told me he couldn't pay me because the guy who escaped took the cash register. So instead, I got a bunch of leftover hot dogs, some beer, and this scarf. It's real nice and comfortable, but you now what? . . . He told me later that he pulled it off that dead guy. Is that some fucked-up shit or what?

U.S. DRAG
Gina Gionfriddo

Comic

Evan (twenties to thirties) is the head of a public awareness group called S.A.F.E., an acronym for "Stay Away From Ed." Ed is a nutcase who has been mugging people in ATM alcoves. Here, he is addressing other members of the group.

EVAN: We are not the police, OK? What we are is a community advocacy and impact group. Our name, which is an acronym, is SAFE. That stands for "Stay Away From Ed."

Basically, we just feel like there's this guy out there like hurting people and the police are just really focused on trying to catch him. Which is great. That's really important. But in putting all their energies into the investigation they're really not attending to our needs and our feelings and our fears as citizens and potential victims.

SAFE is not about catching Ed. That's actually really sort of against our mission statement. Because what we're really about is, you know, staying away from Ed. Keeping SAFE.

We are, again, not a police force. We are a grassroots community impact movement. We are mounting a campaign to increase awareness and keep people safe. . . .

The campaign, which I designed myself, is called — just simply: Don't Help. . . .

As you all know, Ed's MO — or, mode of operation — is to ask his victims for help. He pretends to be sick or handicapped or injured in some way. Typically, he asks for help. His last victim, you recall, acted under the mistaken impression that Ed was blind and needed help punching in his ATM code. Now, I'm sure I don't need to tell you that there was no ATM and there was no bank and that woman — Mary Stone, who is with us tonight — is very lucky to be alive.

Our strategy here is really, really simple. We don't ask anybody to do anything. In fact the only thing we do ask you to do is do nothing. . . .

Don't help. "Just Say No" — if it hadn't been used as an anti-drug slogan — would have worked really nicely, too. But I'm happy with this.

Our goal is to just paper the city with "Don't Help" literature so that people will know just that . . . now is not a good time to help. . . .

Don't help. Decline to connect. We also have . . . "A good Samaritan is a dead Samaritan."

We've got to get the word out. We can make a difference. Because while we may not be able to catch Ed. We can just . . . not help each other and sort of beat him at his own game.

Thanks, you guys.

(Evan makes a "halt" hand gesture and says . . .) SAFE.

U.S. DRAG
Gina Gionfriddo

Comic

> *James (twenties to thirty) is talking to Allison and Angela, two women friends in their twenties who are determined to make as much money as possible, with as little effort as possible. They are part of a public awareness group dedicating to warning people about a serial mugger named Ed.*

JAMES: Like Angela, I am not, by nature, quick to tears. I have cultivated . . . over years . . . a ritual for release. I take a book from my shelf. A murder book. I turn to the center and I see the photographs of the victims. I say their names. I imagine their last moments, their lost promise. I say their names. All of the prostitutes slain in Seattle who lost first their dignity and then their lives and saw no justice. Wendy, Gisele, Theresa, Virginia. I say their names and the tears come. Marcia, Amina, Opal, Denise. I imagine how they must have felt when they knew they were lost . . . Debra, Leann, Constance, Maureen. I break; I sob. *(Pause.)*

I cried for Ed's victims this morning. I didn't have their pictures, but I didn't need them. I know these people. These people were unhappy. Have you ever asked a favor on the street? Have you? Change for a dollar or can I share your cab? Everyone is too busy, too full. These people were lacking. They had moments to spare. They did not have friends or lovers awaiting their arrival. ED IS PREYING ON THE INCOMPLETE and I won't have it!

WHAT DIDN'T HAPPEN
Christopher Shinn

Dramatic

Peter is a rather cynical writer in his forties. He has been invited for the weekend to the country home of David, a writer as well. He is fond of hearing himself talk, and of his opinions, which he considers very trenchant.

PETER: Speaking of pathology, I'd like to lay David on the couch for a moment. May I, David? . . .

Thank you. We're in the market just now, buying some meat, and I remark, "That's a very nice shirt, David." "Yes," he says, "isn't it? But I bought it from Banana Republic and I can't shop there anymore because they use sweatshop labor." . . .

— It's the same thing at cocktail parties, when I hear people speaking in serious hushed tones about Bosnia. "I can't believe we're not doing anything more," they say. "We should be doing something." We, *we?* It's "they" who do things — governments, corporations, "we" have no "power," no effect on history that way, what's all the "we" talk? . . .

— But we just elected a president who went on *Sixty Minutes* with his wife in a headband and told us he was a bad man in his "personal behavior," and we voted for him anyway. I think that's progress! (Lucky she wore that ugly castrating thing, else people might not have sympathized.) But really, it's a new age, and you just have to resign yourself to it, David: we're small creatures in a vast, unfathomable world, a world that spins forward despite us, and whether or not one buys a shirt at Banana Republic is a superfluous dilemma. The shirt is made! What we don't have control over: *that* is history. What we *do* have control over: that is *pleasure.*

WHAT DIDN'T HAPPEN
Christopher Shinn

Dramatic

Alan, a college professor in his forties to fifties, has been invited for the weekend to the home of a writer friend. Here, he is talking to Elaine, another guest, who is a professional actress.

ALAN: — Well, the *Internet!* Do you know it? . . .

It's this mysterious invention, and Columbia has given it to us. . . .

One day, there it appeared, not a word of debate or warning — "Here you are, process or perish!" . . .

Well, my students: my cream-of-the-crop, Ivy League graduate students: there they sat, before class, in the brand-new computer lab — chins at their chests, eyeballs ablaze, entirely at attention! . . .

Read nothing, now nothing, but give 'em a mouse and clickety-click, clickety-click, there's no tearing them away! Do you know one of my students thought World War II happened in the 1920s? To get through my lecture without a snowballing sense of absolute *doom* — However will our world survive with a bunch of smug, ignorant *fools* inheriting — . . .

Oh — You're right. I've had far too much to dr — it's merely change — and thinking of my life — my wife — usually she'd accompany me on a night like this — I'm just worrying over my *own* mortality — *mortality* — the world will be just fine I'm sure — progress always happen in a straight — but — people who once upon a time would have come to me — and spoken to another human being about a dream they'd had — now they may just take a pill . . . — And what, what if everyone agrees that it *is* merely chemical? Worse, what if it really *is?* Then it's — the end — of all I have devoted my life to, all I *believe* in — art — the soul — memory — contemplation . . . What dark times we live in! Darker for the fact that no one acknowledges how dark indeed they are!

WHAT DIDN'T HAPPEN
Christopher Shinn

Dramatic

Peter, a cynical writer in his forties, is visiting another writer at his country home. Here, he is talking to Scott, a college student who is working for his host as an assistant.

PETER: Come over and talk to me, I'm sad. . . .

You really read *Tall Grass?* . . .

When they were arranging my book tour, I told them I wanted to branch out — develop a bigger audience, so I told them not to send me to Boston and LA and Chicago. The real reason was that I was ashamed of the book. I went to cities like Pittsburgh and Ann Arbor, where I knew no one. I was also really fat. — Oh, hey. He didn't mean that. He was angry at *me.* . . .

Well. I am in. Minneapolis. I give my reading. Afterwards, a middle-aged woman — a bit softer than middle-aged actually, but no longer young — this woman — who is black — approaches me. With a big bright nervous face. And tells me how much my books mean to her. I'm aghast, as I've never before been approached by a black reader. I ask her why she likes my books and she laughs as though it's just a preposterous question. "Because they're good. They make me cry," she says.

I want to know more, so I say, "But why?" I'm thinking, What does this woman relate to in my work? My books are about rich white people. She says, "Same shit goes on where I work, people hurting each other, stabbing each other in the back, this one slept with that one, this one's treating that one wrong, and everyone's doing their best but it just falls apart, and it's left like that, no way to put it back together."

So, I invite her to walk with me to my hotel. She does. I say,

"Come to my room and have a cup of tea." She comes in. I make tea. We sit at the cheap shiny coffee table. I say, "I'd like to kiss you." And, quite calmly, quite sweetly, not an ounce of condescension in her voice: she says, "I think you'll be just fine in a few minutes for not having done that." And she smiles an extraordinary smile. As do I. And she is gone.

Because. Do you? . . . For so many years I felt. Doubt and. *Guilt.* Over my work — over my life. And to see — as I sat there with her — ghost — in the room. I thought of her wisdom. Which so eclipsed mine.

Do you see? . . .

That all of "this." *(Gesturing to the porch.)* These "questions" of. — I had written a book from my heart, and that — that made it a good and worthy book. And me a good and worthy man. I have a beautiful wife and a beautiful son. And a loyal reader, somewhere in Minneapolis. I am blessed. My silly life — "The Bourgeoisie and Me." A blessing. And it is so easy. It is that easy to be — *fine.* . . .

In my best moments, I still feel that way. And that's — that's all I really wanted to say.

(Peter turns around briefly, looks at the silent house.)

A wise man would make his exit now.

(Turns back around.)

I'll pretend I am one.

WHERE'S MY MONEY?
John Patrick Shanley

Comic

*Sidney is a rather cynical divorce lawyer (thirties to forties). Henry has
confided his marital problems to him, and now he's thinking of Henry
as a potential client.*

SIDNEY: . . . My first wife flew on planes to fuck men. She would go vast
distances and miss meals to bang a busboy in Council Bluffs. It was
my fault. That was my job. And I didn't do it. I indulged in moral
luxury. I was a wifely husband. And that ain't the job. . . .

Manhood. . . .

It's a job. Done right, it's a tiring job. And women have a lot to
do with what that entails. Sure, women create. The womb. We all
acknowledge the womb. But there's another side. And it's not pretty.
There's a Hindu deity in India named Kali. The god of destruction.
It's a woman. She's got a bloody sword and an appetite for decapi-
tation. In the West, we call her "The Devouring Mother." Creation,
destruction. Every woman has these two sides to her, and every man
must deal with these two sides. Creation, destruction. You gotta ori-
ent a woman in such a way so as to be facing her creative parts. You
want the creative parts. The destructive parts . . . You want those to
be facing away. Toward a wall or an enemy or something. Women
consume, and they must be directed what to consume, or they may
identify you as lunch. You've gotta point them. Like you would a
bazooka. Like you would a chainsaw. You don't hold a chainsaw by
the chain. Let me pull it together another way. Monogamy is like a
forty-watt bulb. It works, but it's not enough. Women used to come
with goats and textiles. When they got upset, they worked on their
textiles and they yelled at their goats. Now they look around, no goats,
no textiles. All there is is some schmuck trying to read his newspaper. All right, all right, here it is boiled down to nothing. Don't bet
the farm, Henry. That's what I'm trying to say. 'Cause if a woman
smells that you're betting the farm on her, you're gonna lose the farm.

WORLD OF MIRTH
Murphy Guyer

Seriocomic

Sweeney (could be any age, thirties to fifties) works in a carny sideshow. He's the clown part of the "Clown Dunk." He sits on a perch and paying customers throw balls at a target. If they hit it, he's dumped in a vat of water. Here, he's shooting the breeze with Emmett, an addled, elderly man who's sort of a hanger-on at the carnival.

SWEENEY: . . . If people did it half as much as they talked about it — You think of all the words that have been spent on love, all the poems? All the songs? And every one of 'em written by somebody sittin' alone. . . .

I don't know, Em. I don't even know what it is anymore. . . .

. . . A girl comes along, wipes the blood off your face, and you think maybe *this* is love. But then you find out she's bleeding even worse than you are. And all you feel is sad. But that ain't love. That's just pity. So you push her to fight back. 'Cause you don't want to feel just pity. But she can't. She's afraid to even try. And pushin' her only makes her cry. So all you can do is hold her. And hate the world for bein' so pitiful . . . When Oscar went out to ask those handicapped people to leave? They told him he was bein' used. He tried to tell them he wasn't, that he *liked* doin' what he did, but they wouldn't listen. One guy kept tryin' to give him a job fixin' air conditioners. Finally Oscar got so fed up he told him to go fuck his air conditioners. Thought the guy was gonna cry. But instead he looked up with this sticky-sweet smile and said, "I love you Oscar." Next thing ya know they're *all* sayin' it. Screamin' it. "We love you Oscar, we love you!" It's love like that that makes you wanna kill somebody. . . .

People so busy bein' in love, they don't even know who they're in love with. "I talk to you when I'm alone." Girl might as well be wearin' a mirror on her face. Everybody braggin' about how much they loved Oscar. Where was all that love when I asked 'em for a few dollars to keep him on the lot? . . .

. . . If you love somebody, you *find* the money. You sacrifice something. That's what love *is*. If love doesn't cost you anything, it's not worth anything. They had the money. Christ, half of 'em spend more on cigarettes in a week. They just didn't want to give it. 'Cause their love is bullshit. So Oscar's dead . . . and I got nobody to talk to.

WORLD OF MIRTH
Murphy Guyer

Dramatic

Kaspar (forties to fifties) is the owner of a rather seedy carnival. Sweeney, a clown whose act was to get dunked by paying customers in a vat of water, has died — possibly murder, possibly suicide — and Kaspar wants to know what happened. Here, he is interrogating a young stagehand, Augie.

KASPAR: Of course you didn't kill him. *I* know that. I know that because I know *you*. But these people comin' in here, they *don't* know you. And the fact is, you *did* trip that target. And you *did* tell Sweeney you were gonna kill him. Those are the facts, Augie. And they don't look good. Now I'm sure Patch has no intention of repeating what he heard. But if he finds out that you're goin' to the police with these wild accusations — and that's all the hell they are — well then I couldn't predict *what* he's gonna do. We take care of our own here, Augie. We have a problem we settle it here. We don't take it off the midway. That includes you, and that includes Patch. It would've included Sweeney, but Sweeney didn't *want* to be included. Sweeney was a troublemaker, Augie. You know that as well as I do. Why would a sweet girl like Marcey run off with a drunk like Sweeney? Does that sound like the Marcey *you* know? It doesn't sound like the Marcey *I* know. And if you really cared about her I would've thought you'd give her more credit than that. Yeah, I'll look into it. But I'll tell you right now what I'm gonna find. Nothin'. Because Sweeney had only one thing he could do well. He had a talent for making lies sound like truth. For making you doubt your own heart. But lies are lies, Augie. No matter how true they may sound. And the heart doesn't lie.

PERMISSION ACKNOWLEDGMENTS

THE FATHER CLOCK by Walter Wykes Copyright 2000 by Lauren Friesen. Reprinted by permission of Dramatic Publishing. Inquiries pertaining to performance rights may be addressed to Dramatic Publishing, 311 Washington St., Woodstock, IL 60098, 815-338-7170 (ph), 815-338-8981 (fx). The entire text of *The Father Clock* has been published by Dramatic Publishing in *Best Student One Acts, Vol. 4.*

FORTUNE'S FOOL by Ivan Turgenev. Adapted by Mike Poulton. Copyright 2002 by Mike Poulton. Reprinted by permission of Alan Brodie Representation Ltd., 211 Picadilly, London W1J 9HF, Great Britain. All rights reserved. The entire text of *Fortune's Fool* has been published in an acting edition by Samuel French Ltd.

FOUR by Christopher Shinn Copyright 2002 by Christopher Shinn. Reprinted by permission of John Buzzetti, The Gersh Agency, 41 Madison Ave., New York, NY 10010. All rights reserved. CAUTION: Professionals and amateurs are hereby warned that *Four* is subject to a royalty. It is fully protected under the copyright laws of the United States of America, and of all countries covered by the International Copyright Union (including the Dominion of Canada and the rest of the British Commonwealth), and of all countries covered by the Pan-American Copyright Convention and the Universal Copyright Convention, the Berne Convention and of all countries with which the United States has reciprocal copyright relations. All rights, including professional, amateur, motion picture, recitation, lecturing, public reading, radio broadcasting, television, video or sound taping, all other forms of mechanical or electronic reproduction, such as information storage and retrieval systems and photocopying, and the rights of translation into foreign languages, are strictly reserved. Particular emphasis is placed upon the question of readings, permission for which must be secured from the author's agent in writing. Inquiries concerning all rights in the play should be addressed to John Buzzetti, The Gersh Agency, 41 Madison Ave., 33rd Floor, New York, NY 10010. This play is a work of the author's imagination. Names and characters either are a product of the author's imagination or are used fictitiously. References to real people are used only to convey the author's satirical purpose and are not to be taken literally. The entire text of *Four* has been published in an acting edition by Dramatists Play Service.

GOOD BUSINESS by Tom Gannon Copyright 2000 by Lauren Friesen. Reprinted by permission of Dramatic Publishing. All rights reserved. Inquiries pertaining to performance rights may be addressed to: Dramatic Publishing, 311

U.S. Drag has been published by Smith and Kraus, Inc. in *Women Playwrights: The Best Plays of 2002.*